TURBO CHARGED STRATEGY

LAURENCE SMITH
Sequel to *Why Strategies Fail*

www.chasenoble.com

"Smith presents us with a strategic compass, fortified with a kaleidoscope of fact-based illustrations, giving a contextual richness to this contemporary read."
Peter Bradley, President, Stryker Japan

"Smith's books, like his consulting reports, sizzle with energy. Ideas explode off every page."
Steve Ferrari, IT and Operations Director, Family Investments

"Like an archaeologist excavating a newly discovered site, Smith approaches strategy by sweeping aside the debris and rubble to unearth the treasures hidden beneath."
Andrew Fisher, Chief Executive Officer, Towry

"An eloquent, thought-provoking, insightful and, above all, action-generating publication. It provides not just the stepping stones towards genuine strategic differentiation, but also case studies that interest and inspire."
Stephen Gates, Managing Director, Denplan

"Running a company can be a lonely business when it comes to strategy and decision-making. Working with Smith helps me to see the direction of my company in a clear way, build a strategy that's practical, and act quickly to address challenges."
Charlie Haynes, Chief Executive Officer, Marketing Punch

"Smith has a creative, intuitive approach to strategy – he knows how to peel the proverbial skin off the onion and get to the heart of the issue."
**Guy Hollis, Executive Director
and EMEA Head of Markets Developments, CBRE**

"Occasionally stubborn, often tenacious, always focused. Smith certainly knows how to get the job done!"
Steve Jenkins, Director - Financial Services and Insurance Markets, Chartered Insurance Institute

"TurboCharged he was, and TurboCharged he remains. I often return to the mode of thinking of this great strategist. Working with Smith was always an inspiration, an adventure, a whirlwind of lateral ideas and a window to thinking outside the box."
Amanda Johnson, Chief Executive Officer, Active Learning Childcare

"For 25 years, I've seen Smith display passion for business, creative ideas for strategic growth, and now wisdom and experience. His books are a 'must read' for anybody seriously interested in taking their organisation to the next level."
Martin Leuw, Chief Executive Officer (fmr), IRIS Software Group

"Whether he's analysing the growing pains that face entrepreneurs, or the challenges that confront you once you're established, Smith's books teem with tips and insight."
Mark Norgate, Managing Director, Donnington Strategic Land

"Put Smith in front of a focus group, and watch the participants come alive. Creative ideas flow with abandon. Always fun and fast, with the emphasis on fun."
Chrissie Rogowska, Partner, Wanford Fieldwork Partnership

"M&A strategy can be an alien process leaving business owners feeling isolated and at sea. So Smith's guidance, expertise, experience and realism has been an invaluable asset. It would be a much more stressful journey without him."
Dr Anthony Walsh, Chairman and Medical Director, the Sims Group

This edition first published 2013.

Copyright © Chase Noble Ltd, 2013.

Published by Chase Noble Ltd. Registered office Audley House, Brimpton Common, Berkshire RG7 4RT.

Illustrations by Kev F Sutherland.

Designed by Rita Sexton.

Printed by Hobbs The Printers, Hampshire

British Library Cataloguing in Publication Data. A catalogue record for this book is available from the British Library.

ISBN 978-0-9575092-1-4.

Dedicated to my first-born
Alex

Keep On Howlin'!

\

CONTENTS: INSIDE THE TURBOCHARGER

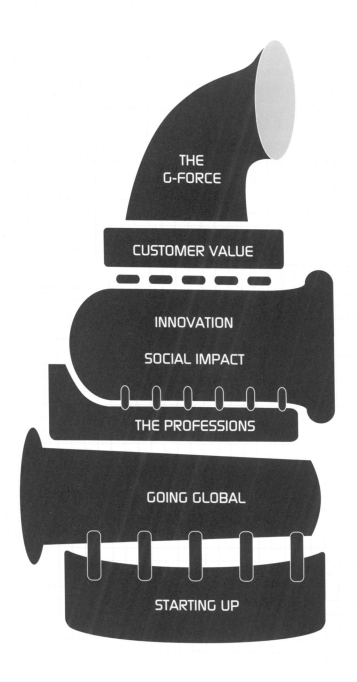

ACKNOWLEDGEMENTS

TIME IS A precious asset, and comes at a particular premium for hard-pressed business leaders. I'm grateful for all those who gave up many hours to be interviewed as part of the research phase of this book. Without their insights and wisdom, my task would have been nigh impossible.

In particular, I would like to express my appreciation to Gabi Blumberg (Social Impact Manager, The Good Analyst), Simon Carpenter (Head of Insight, Zurich Global Life), Amy Clarke (Head of Advisory, Charities Aid Foundation), Cabell de Marcellus (Chief Technology Officer and Co-Founder, Dianomi), Kenton Fine (Group Chairman, Servest), Ian Fletcher Price (Chief Executive Officer, Posturite), Lance Forman (Chief Executive Officer, H Forman & Son), Dr Richard Friedland (Chief Executive Officer, Netcare), Andy Friedman (Chief Executive Officer, Professional Associations Research Network), Anne Godfrey (Chief Executive Officer, Chartered Institute of Marketing), Jeremy Greenhalgh (Chief Investment Officer, Innervation Capital Partners), Suzanne Hardy (Community Investment Specialist, Network Rail), Catherine Hill (Marketing Director, Chartered Institute of Purchasing and Supply), Jonathan Jenkins (Chief Executive Officer, The Social Investment Business Group), David Kaufman (Senior Managing Director, Envest Ventures), Adrian Moore (Technical Director, Xtrac), David Neenan (President – International, TransUnion), David Noble (Chief Executive Officer, Chartered Institute of Purchasing and Supply), Peter Owen (former Director of Operations, British Airways), Simon Rhodes (EMEA Marketing Director, CBRE), Tim Sawyer (Chief Executive Officer, Start-Up Loans), Dr Sandy Scott (Chief Executive Officer, Chartered Insurance Institute), Susan Scott-Parker OBE (Chief Executive Officer, Business Disability Forum), Michael Smith (Head of Information Technology, Dianomi), Neil Stevenson (Executive Director – Brand, ACCA: the Association of Chartered Certified Accountants), Ashley Sweetland MBE (former Chair of the Trustees, UK Youth Parliament), Sean Tompkins (Chief Executive Officer, Royal Institution of Chartered Surveyors), Chrissie Twigg (Founder and Director, Healthier Weight Centres), Theresa Wallis (Owner, Luella Linen), Paul Warminger (Bid Director, Arqiva), Jerel Whittingham (Director, Kromek), Alistair Wickens (Group Chief Executive, Road To Health), David Wolfe (Chief Executive Officer, Brand Journey) and Stephen Wynne-Jones (Head of Marketing Operations, Cofunds); as well as participants in the Enterprise 500 Programme including Tali Shlomo (Programme Champion), Katie Bowers, David da Costa, Nicola Pope, Jacob Quagliozzi, Joanna Shortt and Suzanne Townsend.

Each one provided a wealth of shrewd observations, expressed with verve and passion, and supported by an abundance of personal examples that often challenged my prior assumptions. With some of these interviewees, it was a delight to renew an acquaintanceship after too long. With others, we were meeting for the first time. But they all had one thing in common: they were open in their inferences and honest in their convictions. In the interests of full disclosure: a few of the interviewees have been consulting clients of mine, Michael Smith is my brother, and Theresa Wallis is my wife.

Graphic designer, Rita Sexton, once again used her discerning eye and rich imagination to take my manuscript and transform it into a professional end-product. Having set a high bar with her previous creations, this time she smacked it clean out of the park. Kev Sutherland's illustrations in my last book proved hugely popular, so I'm grateful for his return to these pages; his cartoons are again captivating and poignant. And welcome to a couple of newcomers. Will Martyr, alumnus of the Slade School of Fine Art and the Royal College of Art, created a front cover image of intensity and bombast; and Michele Brailsford proofread with grace and gusto to rid my scribblings of the most egregious errors, repetitions and non sequiturs.

My thanks to Kathleen Garwood, Jamie Heath, Tamsin Mills, Owen Morgan and Paul Turner, who read parts or all of the manuscript prior to publication and made a number of valued suggestions. To Juliet Brilliant, Darren Garner and Steve Hunter, who between them introduced me to a number of excellent interviewees I would otherwise not have encountered. And to Mark Hutchinson and David Ross, whose enthusiastic promotion of the previous volume helped to motivate this sequel.

As I storm ahead with this latest madcap scheme, I'm acutely conscious that being a member of my household is not for the faint-hearted. Thank you again to Theresa and the boys for tolerating me and supporting each other while I've been sequestered away, fretting over the coming words.

FOREWORD

TINA TURNER'S SIGNATURE rock anthem, from her 1989 solo album *Foreign Affair*, has been adopted as a motivational theme tune by world champions from boxer, Chris Eubank, to Formula One legend, Ayrton Senna, This would not have happened if the iconic singer had caveated her assertion. If – instead of belting out "You're simply the best" – she had more hesitantly suggested "You're simply ... in the top few percentiles."

For high achievers such as Eubank and Senna, success isn't about keeping up with the pack. For them, a top three finish is inadequate. The winners' podium reserves one solitary step for the gold medallist. A world record is viewed, not as the pinnacle of success, but as a stepping stone en route to greater triumph. Such individuals see history as a grand tapestry, recording the human race's endeavours down the centuries to be stronger, richer, faster, bigger.

When high achievers pick up a prototype, they don't gaze at it with puppy-eyed, passive admiration. Their minds are already feverishly re-engineering each component to stretch performance further, challenging constraints and pushing against limits.

It wasn't long after the invention of the internal combustion engine that scientists were subjecting its basic configuration to this type of interrogation. For a naturally aspirated engine of given dimensions, they pondered, what methods existed to take power and efficiency to a higher level? When Swiss engineer, Alfred Buchi, created a forced induction device that propelled more air, and therefore more fuel, into the combustion chamber, he took a breakthrough invention, which was already in the process of revolutionising long-established patterns of work and leisure, and with inspiration and knowledge added a further twist. Thus was born the turbocharger.

Buchi's flair has never been more relevant than today, when – as in the early 20th century – we face the emergence of a dazzling and unsettling new world. Business strategies which once passed muster are now woefully inadequate. In this book, I have selected seven areas where the inherited methods no longer suffice and subjected them to a Buchi-like glare. In the process, I offer a few principles which, I trust, may interest any reader wrestling with a strategic dilemma and striving to turbocharge the future.

In *Why Strategies Fail*, I recommended 17 tactics that managers can use to avoid falling waist deep into quicksand. But the avoidance of danger merely delays the terror of the eventual reckoning. *TurboCharged Strategy* is about looking beyond immediate survival. It's about being not merely moderately noteworthy or simply satisfactory, but – to borrow Tina's immortal phrase – "the best".

KNOWING YOUR PIVOT POINT

TOP OF THE list of driving skills for gargantuan road vehicles, according to Mark Polk of the United States Family Motor Coach Association, is to *know your pivot point*. He asserts drily, "If a tree is ahead of your pivot point, and you turn your vehicle towards it, you will hit it." As a metaphor for developing and implementing organisational strategy, it functions on multiple levels.

TurboCharged strategists understand how to pivot. The organisation may have sauntered (like a motor coach) in the shadows, manoeuvring through narrow back streets, picking up passengers and topping up the fuel. It's now emerging from the dark. It's about to ascend to the expressway, heading full throttle towards a new landscape. As the strategist prepares to crank up the power, energies and focus will be directed at executing a perfect pivot. At this point, historic baggage will be jettisoned; a beckoning future awaits.

Jeremy Greenhalgh has been one of London's most successful private equity leaders for the past 20 years. As a founding partner at *Charterhouse Capital Partners*, he was involved in eight funds totalling £12 billion as the sector evolved from its origins (buying out unloved orphan assets from conglomerates), to the early 2000s heyday era of the mega deal. He is now raising funds for a new venture, *Innervation Capital Partners*, which will back management teams facing an opportunity, perhaps time-limited, to capture value in fast-changing sectors, and drive performance improvement through sector focus.

For Greenhalgh, pivot points are critical to a successful investment. "I'm looking for the potential and capability to realise an asymmetric return," he comments. "This means downside protection for sure, but crucially an opportunity to move the needle on the upside. A management team with a clear view of their pivot point gives me a lot of comfort. I look for leaders that understand when and how this inflection will happen, and – when it does – can direct their resources, with uncompromised intensity, to exploit it."

Pivot points may involve a change in regulation, for example the recent liberalisation of the gaming industry, or in new customer behaviours, such as the ways ageing baby-boomers are addressing their healthcare needs, or in transforming technologies, with the emergence of cheap data creating new service opportunities for outsourcers. "I call these value creation scenarios," says Greenhalgh. "They are distinct from the value capture model, which is where much of private equity is now headed. Value capture is about building portfolios where large amounts of capital can be deployed with minimal volatility around the returns. You concentrate on derisking, and forego the home runs. Value creation moves the curve to the right."

Exploiting pivot points means that value creation investors can still achieve high multiple upsides (see *Figure 0.1*). They eschew incremental improvement and shun baby steps. "Proprietary off-market deal flows. Niche breakthroughs that can be taken into product or geographical adjacencies. Companies that can be repositioned, revalued or rerated under new ownership. Fragmented industries where no one has built the platform for consolidation. These are all interesting types of pivots," observes Greenhalgh.

FIGURE 0.1: Value creation strategies and pivot points

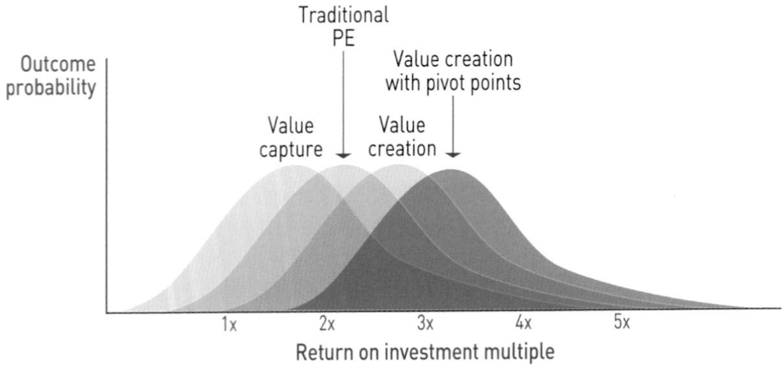

Source: Innovation Capital Partners/Chase Noble

TurboCharged Strategy investigates the ways that strategists, facing 21st century challenges, can apply the principles of the pivot point to rethink how they tackle the road ahead. I trust it will be of value to all those seeking a navigable route through to a brighter tomorrow.

For the start-up (Chapter 1), the pivot may be determining which of three strategies will be employed to battle against incumbents – cost efficiency in commoditised sectors, substitute solutions that tap into existing markets, or new products which catalyst fresh demand. For the global enterprise (Chapter 2), the pivot could be forging a business model that harnesses cross-border and cross-cultural capabilities and enables them to be deployed locally. For the professions (Chapter 3), the pivot might be transforming how competence, conduct and culture are manifest in an age of cynicism, focusing increasingly on the application of knowledge and the delivery of a public interest benefit.

For social entrepreneurs (Chapter 4), the pivot might be substituting the paternalist definition to philanthropy with a model based on investment, impact and measurement. For innovators (Chapter 5), the pivot may be decoupling new thinking from the shackles of business-as-usual through the combustible mix of a clear and audacious vision, formidable resourcing, a bogeyman to spur change, and theorists working alongside practitioners. For value proposition experts (Chapter 6), the pivot could be breaking the traditional trade-off between cost and quality through exerting greater influence over economic value, reinventing the organisation's essence, and restructuring the value chain. And for team leaders (Chapter 7), the pivot might be introducing a G-Force mentality to transform teams into champions.

My scribblings are targeted at strategists in any or all of these camps. As you hit the apex of the tightest hairpin bend, slam the brakes, increase the throttle, and prepare to accelerate with the turbocharger propelling fuel into the chamber like an uncontrollable torrent gushing from a burst dam, I send best wishes for the journey ahead. It's time to hit the open road ... and make history!

STRATEGY AND STARTING UP

Hunting monsters or monkfish

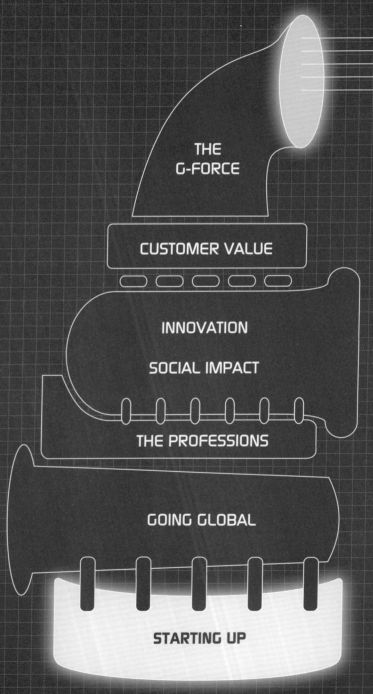

THE
G-FORCE

CUSTOMER VALUE

INNOVATION

SOCIAL IMPACT

THE PROFESSIONS

GOING GLOBAL

STARTING UP

IN THE COMPANY OF GIANTS
(BDO STOY HAYWARD, START UP LOANS)

- An entrepreneurial renaissance is underway
- Outrageous ambition plus unconventional implementation
- The five characteristics of budding tycoons.

THE POWER OF THREE
(ENVEST VENTURES, LUELLA LINEN)

- Traditionally, new entrants are disadvantaged when confronted by a brutal establishment
- Three challenger strategies available to new entrants
  - Cost efficiency in commoditised sectors
  - Substitute solutions tapping into existing markets
  - New products which catalyse new demand
- With the internet age, challenger strategies are more plentiful and viable.

A FLAIR FOR THE DRAMATIC
(SERVEST)

- The lumbering and bureaucratic nature of incumbents
- Time-sensitive opportunities demand theatrical gestures and game-changing plays
- How entrepreneurs shape the future.

ADAPTING TO THRIVE
(HEALTHIER WEIGHT)

- Recognising when the initial offer did not quite cut it
- Sensitivity to market signals and the courage to change course
- The canny intervention of mentors.

FROM START-UP TO PACESETTER
(POSTURITE)

- When hand to mouth no longer suffices
- Breaking through with renewed direction and upgraded priorities
- Lady Fortune is not a meritocrat.

IN THE BREATHLESS opening scenes of the cult 2005 series *Prison Break*, brilliant engineer Michael Schofield (played by Wentworth Miller) is arrested for the attempted armed robbery of a crowded bank in the centre of Chicago, pleads no contest during a hastily convened court hearing, and begins a five-year sentence at the notorious Fox River State Penitentiary. As the sequence concludes, Schofield seemingly faces desperate times, deprived of all his personal effects, and sharing a desolate cell with intimidating fellow inmate, Fernando Sucre.

Only as the plotline unfolds is Schofield's elaborate purpose revealed. His incarceration was deliberate: the unlikely first phase in an intricate plan, requiring 22 episodes to unfold, to free his brother from a sentence of death. His preparations have allowed for multiple variables and scenarios so that, even from the confines of a six by eight foot steel cell, he's always a step ahead of the wardens.

IN THE COMPANY OF GIANTS

When the entrepreneurial vision combines an outrageous ambition, such as Schofield's, with an equally unconventional implementation, is this the mark of inspiration, or of desperation? Is Schofield's headstrong mindset, which makes such compelling viewing in a fictional box set, transferrable to the commercial arena? Are the eccentric schemes of budding tycoons symptomatic of a breakthrough discovery? Have they, in the words of Hungarian Nobel-Prize winner, Albert von Szent-Györgyi, "seen what everybody else has seen and thought what nobody else has thought"? Or, instead, is novelty prone to result in a mouthful of mud?

Almost everyone, at some time, has daydreamed about building a business from scratch, imagining a future where they are feted by admiring politicians, adored by fawning staff, surrounded by hyper-ventilating groupies, and idolised by an indulgent media as they soar ever further up the *Sunday Times* Rich List. Fictional and real-life role models – Richard Branson, Jay Gatsby, John D Rockefeller, Tony Stark – hint at a world of private islands, boundless riches, glamour and excess. However, to take the next step – and convert idle musings into a remorseless destiny – requires an extraordinary disposition.

"I have been astonished by the numbers who are turning their back on traditional career options, preferring the freedom of running their own business," says Tim Sawyer, Chief Executive Officer of *Start-Up Loans*, which was recently established by the government to channel seed finance to entrepreneurs with viable ideas but who are outside the reach of the conventional banking system. "At outset, we were somewhat concerned about whether we could attract sufficient deal flow. But the demand is semi-insatiable." Sawyer sees a number of societal trends that are sparking a revitalisation in Britain's entrepreneurial culture. "The media has certainly played a role," he comments, citing the BBC's *Dragon's Den* as perhaps the most influential example. "But also young people no longer see traditional employment as secure. If they're going to work hard, they think, they'd like to experience the upside, rather than forever fearing dismissal at the arbitrary whim of a corporate boss."

The renewed appeal of risk-taking cuts across a wide range of sectors, as revealed by an analysis of the initiatives financed by Start-Up Loans during its pilot period (*Figure 1.1*). "Nor is it limited to a particular type of person," says Rhiannon Evans, Relationship Manager. "Financing has been offered to graduates from top universities and drop-outs from deprived communities. We have backed people leaving the army, and people leaving jail."

FIGURE 1.1: Industry categories in receipt of financing from Start-Up Loans, 2012

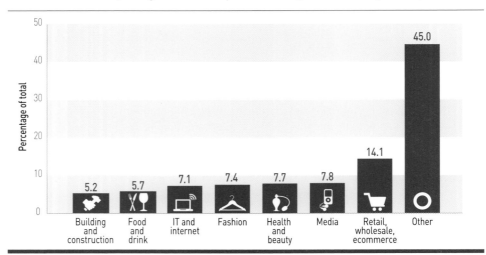

Source: Start-Up Loans

Sawyer adds that, while the demographics of the recipients may vary, one factor is a prerequisite. "We need evidence of motivation," he says. "If the drive and desire doesn't exist, how can I be confident the loan will ever serve a constructive purpose? The evidence of motivation is not necessarily a 42 page plan. But I expect them to answer some basic questions about the idea and their suitability to deliver." Peering into the souls of would-be entrepreneurs is less exact than inspecting the empirical data within a PowerPoint slide pack. It may require the intuition of the gambler coupled with the mind reading powers of the clairvoyant.

The scrutineer will need to judge how the individual will respond to a positive decision: will they head straight to the candy store or tuck away the funds under the mattress? If they are denied capital, will they throw a fit, badger and bicker, or smooth out their rough edges before launching a second attempt? Small wonder that one of the most successful early stage investors of my acquaintance, Paul Hirschbiel (who in 1987 backed a small Texas-based microchip manufacturer called *Dell Computers*) once told me his studies in Child Psychology had been as valuable as his degree in Business Administration.

Before I knew Hirschbiel, I was fortunate enough to enjoy a ringside seat in the 1980s, observing many of that decade's most swashbuckling daredevils from the unlisted sector. *Stoy Hayward*, the accountancy firm where I began my working life, and which is now part of the international BDO network, was focused on supporting mid-sized and family-owned businesses. Almost daily there were opportunities to meet and engage with buccaneering business leaders, who had oftentimes started out with just a fistful of used notes wrestled from sympathetic relatives, and over the years had challenged and reshaped whole sectors.

FROM START-UP TO PACESETTER

Even amongst the start-ups that break through into the big league, the early days are often characterised by short-term, knee-jerk decisions and blind instinct. *Posturite* is now the UK's market leader in the ergonomic equipment sector, with a range of manufactured products and distribution arrangements that encompasses chairs, desks, computer accessories and numerous ancillary categories. Yet its origins lay in a chance encounter.

Founder Ian Fletcher Price explains: "It took me nine years to realise I couldn't play corporate games. When I was fired from the City for the second time, I turned to cabinet making for an income." One of his early clients turned out to be an osteopath, and they started chatting about the problems office workers can face with day-to-day tasks if they suffer from a bad back or poor posture. "He financed my materials for a prototype sloping adjustable board I could take to a Royal Society of Medicine trade show," says Fletcher Price. "I don't think I'd ever been to a trade show before. I don't think I even knew what one was."

Throughout the early years of Posturite, almost every decision was taken to satisfy one over-riding obsession: survival. As with a child's spinning top, the slightest disruption could precipitate a violent topple. Tactics, acumen and nous crowded out any thoughts about the firm's longer term destiny. "It was seat of the pants stuff. If I did something on Monday, it was usually to ensure I could get to Tuesday. We spent our entire time reacting. We'd created a business but it was going nowhere."

Fletcher Price's determination for Posturite to survive meant that, even during those dark days, choices were occasionally made that laid secure foundations. Without consciously taking hold of the firm's destiny, the simple fact of being active in the marketplace meant he would pick up nuances and suggestions, and feel compelled to pursue them. "Customers were asking me what else I had in the range. I asked them what they wanted. They kept saying chairs. So I found them chairs. I could dress this up in hindsight as my product extension programme. But the truth is, it was gut feeling. It was terror that, unless I sorted out their requests, they wouldn't pick up the phone again." Fletcher Price's acute market antennae, and ability to strike a deal, meant a business was gradually taking shape that exhibited diversity of product and client type around the simple, focused concept of a more ergonomically effective workplace.

For seven years, Posturite careened from one opportunity to the next, never over-reaching itself, but never moving beyond its fragile roots. The business remained viable due to ferocious energy, client goodwill and the dedication of family members (Fletcher Price's mother served as a one-woman finance, operations and human resources director). To the casual observer, the business seemed to be serenely gliding along. But, just as the graceful Greek warships of the fourth century BC hid banks of grunting, heaving, exhausted oarsmen, so beneath the surface at Posturite was a team paddling furiously simply to stay afloat.

And, for a time, this way of working seemed to the team completely normal. "In this haze of activity, there was frankly no time to reflect." confesses Fletcher Price. "Plus I didn't even know what a SWOT (strengths, weaknesses, opportunities, threats) analysis was. How can you miss what you don't know exists?" But gradually the realisation came that muddling through could not continue indefinitely. At some point, the business climate might turn hostile, and walking a seven year tightrope had left Posturite exposed and vulnerable even to the most temporary setback.

"That was the eureka moment," explains Fletcher Price. "We had got in a rut, and we didn't have the equipment to get out. Then I realised it is possible to plan, and not spend every day reacting and warding off the latest crisis." Over a two month period, supported by his closest associates and colleagues, he sketched out a roadmap for how the business should evolve – stretching its capabilities into complementary areas, upping the tempo of brand noise, and broadening its reach geographically and sectorally. "Since inception, I had been the only salesperson. This meant growth was capped by the number of hours I could physically spend on the road. And I was engrossed operationally and unable to see a bigger picture. I needed clones!"

At the end of the planning exercise, the team reached a consensus on the five medium-term priorities, and set measures for judging progress. "We finally reached maturity. Posturite had partly been my parachute away from the dreaded world of big business. But if we were to be more than a sideshow, we needed to copy some – not all – of those big business structures. The growing pains hurt. I was installing the bureaucracy I'd fled from. But you can't run an organisation with sixty salespeople any other way."

With sales now exceeding £15 million, and with Posturite having metamorphosed from a plucky upstart to part of the ergonomic establishment, every one of the goals in the phase one business plan has been achieved and then some. Fletcher Price's role has evolved by necessity, design and personal preference. With operational responsibilities delegated to the senior management team, his time is spent conceiving the future for Posturite beyond the immediate horizons, and developing the programmes and initiatives to bring this future about. "What are the products that the customers of 2020 will be demanding? Where will the next export markets, not just the obvious one, open up? These are the issues that never received any brainpower when my waking moments were spent bullying some poor property manager to close a deal, and cajoling his accounts department to raise a cheque." With space created for proper strategic leadership, the next phase of growth – to £25 million – is no whimsical dream. "It's very achievable," says Fletcher Price. "It *will* be achieved."

Posturite broke through the glass ceiling. But the failure rate among start-ups can be shocking, especially when they are battered by an adverse economic environment.

Mugshots of grinning teenage Silicon Valley billionaires may hog the covers of the business glossies. But the hordes of embittered almost-rans, muttering into their warm beer about what might have been, go unseen.

According to Shikhar Ghosh, senior lecturer in the *Harvard Entrepreneurial Management Unit*, "failure is the new norm". His research of 2000 early stage enterprises, each receiving at least $1 million in external financing over a six-year period, suggests that around 75 per cent fall short of the projected return on investment. Using a more aggressive definition, the failure rate climbs to over 90 per cent (*Figure 1.5*). The lucre and fame accruing to the minority that surpass expectations are scant consolation to the multitudes who fly too close to the sun, or to the financiers that support their dreams.

FIGURE 1.5: The failure rate of start-ups
US venture backed businesses, 2004-2010

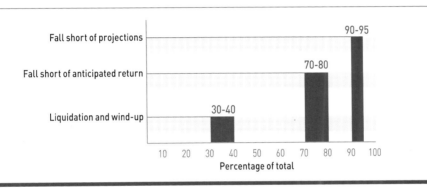

Source: Shikhar Ghosh

Of course, even using Ghosh's metric, failure is far from inevitable, and many early stage investors have defied these pessimistic odds. *The Power Of Three* is a framework for understanding the strategic choices facing newly-launched enterprises. It lays out options for those in charge as they wonder how best to endure the formidable perils of the shallow tributaries and navigate to the faster flowing waterways ahead.

But while a well-engineered strategy may be a prerequisite, in isolation it is woefully insufficient. The entrepreneur must possess the guile and nous to bridge the gulf between theory and practice. He or she must have the emotional intelligence to assemble a management team packed with individuals who work effectively, whether in splendid isolation or as team members. They must have the vision to set priorities, the voice to articulate them, and the dexterity to marshall resources and steer clear of minefields. And they must understand cash flow. "Strategy is superfluous if the firm reaches the end of its financial runway. We've had one of those. It was growing 30 per cent per annum, but if you can't pay for inventory, you can't trade," observes Kaufman.

Most academics and financiers who deal with the sector argue with conviction that a first-rate leader carrying a second-rate idea will enjoy a brighter future than where the qualities are reversed. Michael Schofield eventually frees his brother from Fox River, but not before overcoming setbacks, distractions, treachery, riots, and a spell in solitary that would have devastated a lesser man. In start-ups, as in prison breaks, a premium is attached to dogged perseverance, the ability to inspire and motivate, and the resourcefulness to bounce back unscathed.

The conveyor belt of new enterprises rolls on throughout the business cycle. It is motored by all manner of organised and semi-organised capital, from angels to pension funds. It is piled high with entrepreneurs galvanised by the example of earlier trailblazers, and transfixed by the lure of that coveted fleet of private yachts. The popularity of various strategies may wax and wane; at present, with the outlook far from benign, financiers generally gravitate towards businesses offering cost efficiency or substitute solutions, where the risks are more limited in number and can be more readily dissected. No doubt, when buoyancy returns to the macro-economy, the purse strings will loosen, investors with the strongest track record will aggressively fundraise anew, and the pendulum will swing back towards the game-changers.

HOWEVER, THERE'S A final ingredient that's near impossible to meld into a strategic plan, and that's the arbitrary nature of serendipity. It may be distressing for those who, as if heirs to John Calvin, place paramount store by knowledge, zeal and back-breaking hard graft, but Lady Fortune doesn't seem to be a meritocrat. In start-ups, charismatic chief executives, customer-preoccupied marketers, and engineers who can visualise cutting-edge technologies, may to an extent make their own luck, but the correlation isn't perfect. The history of new firms is littered with vanguard products that, by pure happenstance, faded from view in the shadow of their inferior rivals.

As entrepreneur and journalist Paul Hawken once said: "The luck of having talent is not enough; one must also have a talent for luck." This is one further idiom that, with apologies to Mark McCormack, they don't teach at Harvard Business School.

2 STRATEGY AND GOING GLOBAL
Wanderlust in our DNA

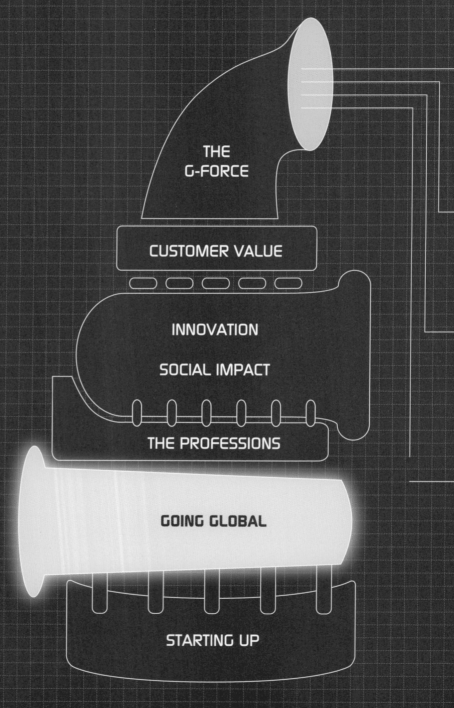

THE
G-FORCE

CUSTOMER VALUE

INNOVATION

SOCIAL IMPACT

THE PROFESSIONS

GOING GLOBAL

STARTING UP

AN URGE TO BREAK FREE

- We're seeing a permanent, seismic shift in how organisations reach across the planet
- The world's financial systems are supporting unprecedented cross-border investment; south-on-south as well as west-on-west
- Gateway cities are dislocating from home countries; for global citizens, geography is fragile and artificial.

SHAPING UP FOR THE MISSION
(BRITISH AIRWAYS)

- An exceptional core business freed from secondary encumbrances
- Unleashing the next generation of intrapreneurs
- The triumph of pragmatic flexibility over rigid orthodoxy.

MANAGING THE GLOBAL BUSINESS
(CBRE)

- Acquisitions can flourish when made for reasons of strategy not grandeur
- Management structures to fuse local accountability with cross-border best practice
- Global brand values designed for local expression

RESPONSIVE TO COMMUNITIES AND CULTURES
(ZURICH)

- Culture is an underrated determinant of attitudes, behaviours, plans
- Community research tools can reveal dramatic and challenging insights
- A global dashboard connects communities, defining attitudinal similarities while reflecting differences
- Everyone benefits when insights are transformed into action

EUROPEAN NEANDERTHALS LED short and grim lives. Their stone tools were crude and unimpressive. They were the dominant but unadventurous inhabitants of the continent for hundreds of thousands of years, but were swept aside – infected or killed – when the Cro-Magnons of Africa developed sufficient wanderlust to explore beyond their inherited lands. With their superior weaponry including bone fishhooks, harpoons, nets and snares, the Cro-Magnons were able to tame colonised territories to their will. They set in motion an era that archaeologists refer to as the Great Leap Forward. The localised and divergent evolution of human populations was being replaced by complex migratory patterns, and within a few thousand years the Neanderthals, like the pre-Clovis tribal settlements in the Americas, were wiped out.

Yet until the dramatic advances in transportation technology of recent centuries, the spread of people and ideas remained constrained by the planet's physical environment. For example, when the wheel was invented circa 3000BC in southwest Asia, knowledge of its functionality spread across Eurasia within centuries, but wheels built independently in Mexico never reached south to the Andes due largely to Mesoamerica's extreme narrowness, especially around modern day Panama. Similarly, the spread of writing systems and animal husbandry methods in the ancient world was haphazard and rarely able to bypass natural obstacles such as deserts, mountain ranges and oceans.

Then came Vasco de Gama, the forerunner of every restless and driven *Fortune 100* chief executive alive today. Charged by the Portuguese King Manuel to open up new trade routes for spices such as cinnamon and nutmeg, de Gama led a 1497 expedition of just four ships and 170 men down the west coast of Africa, round the Cape of Good Hope, and onward to the Indian ocean. Motivated by the riches that could be secured through forging lucrative trade routes, and brutal in his dealings with merchants and competitors, de Gama made three voyages to India over the following decades, and opened the way for successors to reach still further east. His success alerted Portugal's European rivals to likewise seek undiscovered routes and realms. The Age of Exploration had begun.

AN URGE TO BREAK FREE

We seem today to be living through a comparable Great Leap Forward, a permanent and seismic shift in how humans across the planet deal with one another.

A global culture is emerging with startling speed. The *United Nations Educational, Scientific and Cultural Organisation* (UNESCO) has identified that, of 7,000 languages spoken around the world, 2,500 languages are at risk of imminent extinction (46 have but a single speaker). Children now have a richer and broader cultural exposure during their formative years – taught in the classroom alongside expat and immigrant contemporaries, vacationing in a smorgasbord of countries and continents, and enjoying music and cuisine regardless of its origins. Blockbuster Hollywood movies regularly open in China before the United States. Pharmaceutical products are developed by virtual teams of scientists in a dozen time zones, recording their results for instant accessibility in shared folders, located in cyberspace. And a single dishevelled dropout, albeit visionary genius, like Steve Jobs can, within a scant few years, see the nascent concepts he was tinkering with during sleepless Santa Clara Valley weekends mushroom to the point they command a loyal following in almost every city, town and village across the globe.

The globalisation phenomenon would have remained a slow and arduous struggle without the liberalisation of financial markets. Case studies of products (such as Apple's) which have conquered the continents would have remained the exception, not the rule. Monarchs, explorers and the über-wealthy would still be able to satiate their wanderlust, but the bulk of the population would have stayed constrained by the circumstances of their birth. However, within just three decades, capital markets have become genuinely global in their scope, infrastructure and activity. The absolute sums involved have surged tenfold; from a modest $0.4 trillion in 1980 (four per cent of global GDP), they now dramatically account for $4.4 trillion (eight per cent).

One of the earliest and most comprehensive assessments of the unprecedented changes in the functioning of the world's financial nervous system was undertaken by economic consultants, Lowell Bryan and Diana Farrell. More recently, the *International Monetary Fund* (IMF) has addressed the subject in its continuing assessment of ongoing risks to global financial stability. From these various contributions, it seems six factors have been paramount. The ageing demographics of developed economies means a larger cohort of the population hold significant retirement assets from which an income is sought. Investing institutions exhibit less home bias in their asset allocation practices, as they manage the risks of their portfolios. Low interest rates have created liquidity conditions in key financial centres, motivating (argues the IMF) carry trade speculation with little regard to the destination country. Favourable, stable government and regulation in leading financial centres throughout both the developed and developing economies have attracted inward flows. Increased transparency of information means more equal access among market participants, so that issuers, sovereign wealth funds and financial institutions can evaluate options and yields on a global basis, rather than focusing regionally or nationally. And software innovations have enabled the relative risk of opportunities to be modelled and priced using consistent techniques, regardless of origin. Without these enabling trends, the global commercial landscape today would look very different.

In addition to the rising quantum, the *nature* of cross-border capital flows has transformed since the 1980s, from the pseudo-global to the 24-carat global. Funds are no longer funnelled predictably between a few established economies; so-called "west-on-west financing". In just ten years, the share of total cross-border investments accounted for by the United States has fallen from 50 per cent to 32 per cent. In a recent edition of *Mapping Global Capital Markets* by the McKinsey Global Institute, Charles Roxburg and Susan Lund comment on the "south-on-south linkages". Investments between Asia, Latin America, Africa and the Middle East are growing at roughly double the rate of comparable investments from developed countries. Straightforward bilateral financial flows have morphed into a "complex web". China, until recently almost a pariah in the eyes of financial markets, is now the world's second-largest net foreign creditor.

The globalisation adventure has been the catalyst for gateway cities to emerge. The dominant financial centres in each region now exhibit shared characteristics, such as excellent transport infrastructure (airports, proximity to ports or major rivers), large populations with significant employment in financial services and ancillary sectors, and a mercantile tradition. For any corporation with aspirations that require global clout, they have evolved from the hub of choice to the hub of necessity.

Cities such as Frankfurt, Hong Kong, London, New York, Paris and Tokyo already satisfy almost every checklist in the definition of a gateway city. Others, such as Chicago, Dubai, Madrid, Moscow, Mumbai, Rio, San Francisco, Shanghai, Singapore and Sydney, are either investing heavily to join the premier league of global cities, or have arguably already achieved this ranking.

Gateway cities are becoming dislocated from their home markets. Local cultural affinities remain, but often seem quaint or nostalgic alongside their new status as part of a wider global community. The fortunes of, for example, Paris now have more in common with New York and Frankfurt than with Lyon or Marseilles. If one seeks to understand Sydney, then analysis of Hong Kong or London will potentially be more informative than studying Brisbane or Cairns.

As these cities become confident on the global stage, they attract an inordinate volume of capital. A recent CBRE Viewpoint estimated that the proportion of cross-border and inter-regional real estate investment into gateway cities can be as high as 70 per cent. In Central London alone, Real Capital Analytics (RCA) identified that of the 33 major office transactions in 2011, only eight relied upon domestic capital, a further eight used capital from elsewhere in Europe, and the largest tranche involved non-European sources. In three of the largest five transactions, RCA observed, the capital was of Asian origin; from Malaysia (Milton & Shires House), Singapore (Aviva Tower), and Hong Kong (River Court).

Like the eco-system in a Costa Rican rainforest, the global cities are now intricately inter-connected. Rather than seeking one another's extinction, as if they were raw hot-blooded capitalists dreaming of ways to eliminate the competition, they have developed a type of symbiotic dependency. They trade with one another. Skilled and versatile staff move freely between these cities as they advance their careers. Mayors and civic leaders study the practices of counterparts in other gateway cities as they pursue the latest strategies and innovations to cement their profile. From cloud-busting skyscrapers to universal wi-fi, from fiscal incentives to a renaissance in tourism, from sporting arenas to bicycle lanes, from high drama to low comedy, the gateway cities share not just a common ambition, but many of the same fundamentals.

Taking advantage of commercial opportunities from globalisation is not without risk. For every freebooting tale of boundless ambition triumphing over inertia and paranoia, there are a myriad of ill-fated organisations such as the UAE's *Planet Pharmacy* that approach overseas adventures in a zealous spirit of derring-do, and then tumble. For every champagne cork popping at the diversification across borders of revenue mix or the supply chain, there are executives being sacked for overstretch amid recrimination and rancour. Low-hanging fruit must still be picked using a steady hand and with feet planted on terra firma.

FIGURE 2.1: Cross border financial interconnectedness, 1985-2010

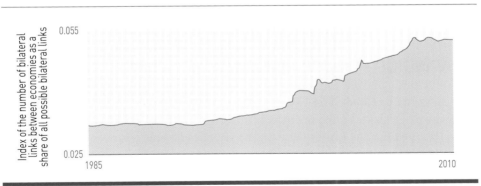

Source: IMF staff estimates, based on Hattori and Suda (2007) and banking sector data from the Bank for International Settlements

Concerned about unanticipated consequences, the International Monetary Fund has developed sophisticated models to stress test the ripple effects of sovereign debt defaults, for example by Eurozone countries, and noted the degree of financial interconnectedness that now exists. "Markets", they argue, "have become more and more inter-linked with each other, particularly since the mid-1990s, as the asset and liability management (ALM) strategies of sovereign financial institutions and corporations have become increasingly global in nature." Their analysis of interconnectedness is shown in *Figure 2.1*, in which the preponderance of bilateral links across the global economy is quantified. In extreme situations, this can increase the vulnerability of the global financial communities, engendering panic and distress if, or rather when, the quality of institutional assets is called into question. But generally, in the IMF's view, the rapid transmission of information from one market to another creates systemic efficiency, and is benign.

With the collapse of cultural barriers, and the convergence of regulation and technology, a class of ultra-mobile global citizens is emerging. Alvin Toffler labelled this trend "the demise of geography" when he described the nomadic lifestyle of skilled workers in his influential work *Future Shock*: "Never in history has distance meant less. Never have man's relationships with place been more numerous, fragile and temporary". Or as Albert Einstein said, in terms that remain colourful and more than a little provocative: "Nationalism is an infantile disease. It is the measles of mankind." Einstein saw himself as a world citizen; his allegiance and loyalties unconstrained by the artificial construct of territorial boundaries; his perspective on contemporary matters defined by the entire planet.

It's clear the urge to break free of boundaries burns as intensely today as when the Cro-Magnons embarked upon their exodus across the Arabian peninsula. The rest of this chapter explores the critical decisions that face strategists and chief executives as they take advantage of increasingly congenial regulatory and financial systems across continents, to lay down their global marker. How do they shape up for the challenge? How should they manage a global business? And, as they pursue their adventures, how can they remain responsive to different communities and cultures?

SHAPING UP FOR THE MISSION

In the aftermath of World War Two, governments realised that bombers such as the B-29 could, with a sprinkling of imagination, be converted into commercial aircraft. From this moment, the reshaping of the planet into a smaller, more familiar, more intimate place was underway. When British state airline BOAC introduced the first commercial jet airliner, the de Havilland Comet, as a scheduled service in 1952, the desire to take to the skies in comfort and safety was no longer a wistful dream. Within 25 years, the average British adult would be taking at least one flight every year. A fantasy had become almost a routine experience during a single generation.

For much of this period, going global for the airlines primarily meant taking people to international places. But by the 1970s and 1980s, globalisation was becoming manifest in an altogether more challenging, more axiomatic manner. With most airlines in state ownership, Cold War governments manipulated their reach to advance geopolitical influence and priorities. And extended families started to travel long-haul not only for vacation or business purposes, but to resettle in new lands. The 200 individuals hurtling at around 500 miles per hour through the skies in a thin steel tube represented, in their glorious diversity of purpose and culture, a microcosm of the entire world stage.

Peter Owen was Director of Operations at *British Airways* in the 1980s, and witnessed these epoch-defining developments firsthand, just as the business model became irrevocably international. "Freed of political interference, one of the first priorities was to internationalise the operation," he explains. "The organisation became more virtual, as we made more imaginative use of third parties." To that point, countless aspects of service were delivered in-house, almost always controlled from London. "It felt too much like the colonial instinct had never faded. The approach was wholly inadequate for the mission we were pursuing."

Under Owen's sponsorship, assets were redirected to those elements of British Airways' operations that enabled it to compete in distant markets for new revenue sources. Functions whose impact upon these strategies was negligible or tangential were variously outsourced, cut back or restructured (the vision of this project was presented in a contemporaneous report and is reproduced in *Figure 2.2*). No option was deemed too radical, if the business case had merit. At Heathrow, the catering centre providing meals for all European flights, was no longer deemed a core function, and passed to new ownership. Likewise the engineering and maintenance of hoists, mobile steps, and baggage carts. Other Heathrow services subject to scrutiny included ground handling, property management, vehicle operations and printing. Immediate savings of over 20 per cent were buttressed with clearer accountabilities and arrangements that allowed new technologies to be driven down the supply chain.

FIGURE 2.2: The principles of a streamlined global airline

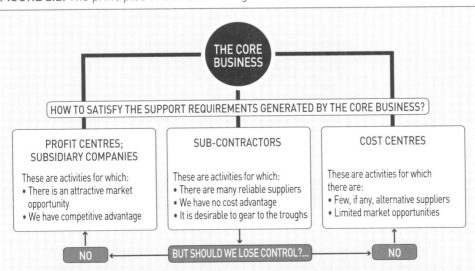

Source: British Airways Operations Review, reproduced in Prime Strategy Consultants position paper 1992

The virtual airline was not, for Owen, an end in itself. "The decision to stop doing certain things meant we freed up capacity for the tasks that mattered." In America, where British Airways was under threat from hub operators out of Atlanta and Charlotte, a fleet of new fuel-efficient aircraft was ordered to reassert the competitiveness of the direct flight. Elsewhere, code sharing and ticket interlining enabled the airline to respond to the needs of passengers with complex flight requirements.

"Management was increasingly planning and investing for the long term," Owen asserts. Route pricing across the globe was taken to a new level of sophistication. The most advanced computations and algorithms in the industry enabled route planning to become more responsive to demand patterns. Commission levels to agents could be flexed in light of a host of factors, from the airline's ambitions in a particular territory to known behaviours within the channel. And pricing, yield management and profitability finally had a modicum of logic and alignment. The long-term thinking was even evidenced in the decision to remove some of the brightest brains on the payroll from their day-to-day responsibilities to, in Owen's words, "Get cracking on Terminal Five. That was back in 1988, 20 years before it opened. I suppose it proves that, in aviation, you can't always achieve your goals overnight, however determined you might be."

British Airways' drive to globalise its service and strategy demanded a new mindset. As a nationalised corporation, managers often rose through the ranks if they were sufficiently nimble to avoid blame, and if they commanded respect within Whitehall for their bureaucratic largesse. Privatisation released the airline from the handcuffs of these obligations. Instinctive subservience to civil service edicts was no longer an essential management capability; instead, the board needed intrapreneurs who would spot opportunities, take responsibility, and be creative. "There was a saying during those times," recalls Owen. "The southern routes were being run like a British public school. The eastern routes like an airline. And only the western routes like a business."

Owen joined the task force of four executives, led by chief executive, Sir Colin Marshall, whose mission was to ensure all routes were operating on sound commercial principles. "This goal could only be achieved by replacing the old guard who saw the airline as an extension of empire with new talent who understood what a service business means." As he set to work to install a new generation of leaders, Owen discovered that in most cases external headhunting was unnecessary. "We had really good people in areas such as Ops Research and Industrial Relations. My task was to give them wings."

As the 1980s drew to a close, British Airways was cementing its position as a global leader in a field littered with national flag-carriers and domestic champions. The arriviste managers proved a handful for senior executives, bombarding them with proposals to change, refocus, acquire, invest and launch. Some concepts were ahead of their time, beyond even the limits of Marshall's perennial revolution. A suggestion that economy class should be rebranded and outsourced to *Poundstretchers* never made it out of the birthing suite. Nevertheless, within five years of its transition to the private sector, the airline had undergone upheaval that was formidable both in its breadth and depth.

For Owen, the most important lesson during this period was that, while certain elements of customer experience could be unified, local sensitivities were plentiful, and abounded in every location where a plane could touch down. "Catering is an obvious point, with the need for halal and kosher meals," says Owen. "But it was more nuanced and varied than food. For example, during those years we often looked after passengers from India who had never been in a train before, let alone an airplane. Imagine how frightening that could be. Our cabin crew were selected and trained to handle very unpredictable situations."

Management was also conscious that only in part were perceptions of British Airways as a global pioneer determined by the on-board experience. Its brand communications was equally significant, and as its international network expanded, it received recognition and awards for the inspirational nature of its marketing. The strapline – *the world's favourite airline* – may have been conceived in aspiration rather than fact, but it caught the public imagination. It became so closely associated with the airline's brand that, for a time, the company toyed with running campaigns that omitted its name and relied exclusively on the catchphrase.

Even with something as seemingly innocuous as an uplifting brand message, it didn't always prove easy to balance global and local pressures. Owen recalls the time he spent as Head of Station in pre-revolution Tehran. "The orthodoxy from London was we should translate what we were given; no other changes were allowed. One day we were given an ad that boasted how well BA took care of Tutankhamun. It would have meant nothing in Iran. All they wanted to know about was the deal. It's a fallacy to think you just have to spend a million dollars on a high profile poster campaign to change the buying habits of the bazaar." Fortunately for Owen, there was no-one in London to back-translate his implementation. "Our cable back to head office confirmed we were dutifully compliant, that the ad paraded the virtues of our meticulous transportation of said Egyptian pharaohs. In fact, in Persian, it boldly screamed 40 per cent off rack rates."

In a world overflowing with fickle, capricious people living in turbulent, erratic communities, going global means pragmatic flexibility must sometimes triumph over rigid orthodoxy.

MANAGING THE GLOBAL BUSINESS

In the past decade, CBRE has forged the world's first truly global full service brand in the real estate sector. Operating in excess of 300 offices worldwide, the firm claims to hold a leadership position in most of the word's key business centres. "We only exist as a global brand because ten years ago the directors of Richard Ellis saw that regional supremacy was becoming irrelevant," comments Simon Rhodes, the firm's ebullient Marketing Director for Europe, the Middle East and Africa. "They were strong in Europe but realised this was insufficient. Merging with CB in the United States was a dramatic change. And was an essential foundation stone for a genuine global future."

Globalisation in CBRE's sector has been driven by a convergence of three factors: client need, shareholder appetite, and market opportunity. The firm's clients include property investors, developers and occupiers who increasingly operate cross-border. Such clients address property portfolio issues without much regard for national borders. Their holdings may variously be located in pristine Californian technology hubs, or bustling conurbations in the Indian subcontinent, or Egyptian resorts. For them, it's business critical to receive real estate advice that considers their complex portfolios on an integrated, not piecemeal, basis.

CBRE's shareholders have also welcomed its emergence as a property advice powerhouse. The legacy of the 2008 financial crisis has been enduring political and economic uncertainty; squeezing out mid-sized practices that are unduly exposed to a limited number of markets, sectors or service lines. Only a firm with critical mass has the scope to balance its investment between transactional services such as leasing or brokerage, and ongoing contractual services such as outsourced property management. This means, uniquely among its peer group, CBRE has been able to exploit a time-limited market opportunity to invest in the long term, while its traditional competitors were distracted by the need to restructure balance sheets or reduce high and inflexible levels of fixed costs.

CBRE's chosen route to a global network has been partly organic expansion, but primarily a relentless programme of strategic and infill acquisitions. In 2006, the firm completed the purchase of the *Trammell Crow Company*, catapulting it ahead of its rivals in its outsourcing service for occupiers. Then, in 2011, it acquired most of *ING Group's* European and Asian real estate investment management operations, as well as the real estate listed securities business based in the United States. During the intervening years, scarcely a quarter would pass without the announcement of a deal to acquire a regional or specialty firm somewhere in the world, or to bring within the group a previous affiliate relationship.

Since 2006, over 60 such deals have been executed for an aggregate investment of over $600 million, expanding CBRE's reach in such diverse territories as Australia, Turkey, Switzerland and Vietnam. "The hunt has been for companies that give us something complementary," says Rhodes. "That make us better, not merely bigger. Often they will bring specialism in a location or a discipline that we previously lacked." For Rhodes, the trouble-free delivery of acquisitions is one instance where success truly breeds success. "It's important to gain a reputation for handling acquisitions professionally and seamlessly. That's when other high calibre firms looking to exit will seek you out."

The acquisition of service businesses, heavily reliant on human capital, has not been without its challenges. Many of the acquired entities thrived in their marketplaces due not to their scale but the guile, versatility and showmanship of the entrepreneurial local team. In fact, clients often warmed to them precisely because they were independent of distant control or faceless bureaucracy. CBRE could ill-afford to wield an indiscriminate corporate sledgehammer and risk the departure or demotivation of respected local personnel. On the other hand, an "anything goes" approach would be incompatible with the principle of consistent global standards demanded by top tier clients, and which comprised some of the strategic rationale for the transaction. Line by line, measure by measure, brick by brick, global standards were being erected and opt-outs were inadmissible.

CBRE's task has been to find that elusive solution – one that could fuse together the dynamic spirit of the local entrepreneur within the disciplines necessary for a joined-up cross-border client offer. Professional judgement was key. A blunderbuss insistence upon uniformity would be as ill-advised as a glib attitude of *laissez-faire*. CBRE needed to find ways to identify the priorities for change. Where did a consistent approach add greatest value? And where could authority be delegated and subsidiarity encouraged? Could it harness best practice, and deploy it in ways that responded to market factors on a town, city or country basis. "Above all," comments Rhodes, "we had to persuade in-county leaders that commitment to shared best practice is ultimately in their own best interests. Would they believe that a more integrated firm isn't incompatible with local success, but in fact its guarantor?"

To advance this cause, in recent years CBRE has created a series of cross-border groups. Some of these function at a global level, and involve collaboration between the leaders of the three major regions (the Americas, Asia Pacific, and Europe, the Middle East and Africa). Some work at a regional level, and include the heads of the key territories. The cross-border groups are structured around the firm's technical disciplines – leasing, property management, valuation, capital markets, building consultancy – and in each case are headed by a seasoned professional, respected for his or her track record and willingness to set aside partisan interests.

"The groups are consciously designed to function through the power of influence, argument and consensus, rather than diktat," says Rhodes. Except *in extremis*, and in matters related to standards, they cannot impose their will by decree since in-country experts still report through to the local managing director, who has undiminished accountability for the financial health of the local business. But the managing director is expected to pay honest heed to any recommendations proffered from the cross-border group, for example about recruitment and ramping up. "Moreover, the influence has corporate teeth," adds Rhodes. The cross-border groups report through to a board member who can take up and champion issues on the rare occasion that differences of opinion between the cross-border and in-country perspective cannot be resolved at the sharp end.

"We have reached a point where the ability to operate internationally isn't optional. It's actually a core competence when you're at a certain level of seniority," Rhodes adds. "There are so many cross-border links. We have cross-border clients, cross-border processes, cross-border working groups, cross-border programmes. Collaborative behaviour is vital, even when it means foregoing what might be in your best short-term local interest because of the wider good."

Cross-border priorities such as client development, service development, and thought leadership are drawn into the open through the annual strategic planning cycle. Each cross-border head is charged with developing and documenting a record of how the bar will be raised over the coming year.

The plans (which follow a set framework) commence with an environmental analysis. The latest data of market trends and opportunities must be obtained to inform a full and frank discussion about opportunities and threats. They include an assessment of CBRE's current market position in each territory, defined by share, market position, growth trajectory, and reputation. They set out the client proposition, with succinct statements to capture the nature of the service being provided, the target market being addressed, the benefit being delivered, the differentiation being claimed, and the communication channels being accessed. They document the cross-border group's strategic objectives and how these translate into specific, measurable, time-bound actions for the year ahead. And they pull together the disparate threads into an overarching theme for the year, so that the attentions of everyone within the service line can be centred around a common narrative. In the current wave of plans, strategic objectives include the further development of the platform through acquisition, a talent strike programme to entice high-flyers to join CBRE, deployment of worldwide technology to support the property valuation process, and innovative tools to augment online office search.

The content of these plans are devised through interaction rather than decree. Each cross-border head works with a Strategic Executive of the most experienced heads of business through the region to sift, probe and test ideas, Members of the Executive speak regularly via conference call, and meet in person up to three times each year.

With the objectives defined, the Strategic Executive also monitors progress against delivery. For each service line, a dashboard of measures is agreed and cascaded from regional, to country, to office and (sometimes) to individual level. Crucially, the measures are not weighted disproportionately in favour of the financial metrics. Matrix management can sometimes become unbalanced through excessive concentration on profit and loss at the risk of complementary factors. In CBRE's case, measures under the headings of people, market position, clients, business development, standards and thought leadership, are all used to offset this risk. *Figure 2.3* contains an extract from CBRE's checklist of cross-border indicators to which Strategic Executive members are now signed up.

FIGURE 2.3: Selected cross-border performance measures in place at CBRE

Financial	• Revenue • Revenue by service type	• Revenue by client type • Revenue by asset type
People	• Headcount • Strategic hires	• Training and development
Market position	• Market share • Countries where #1	• Countries where top 3
Clients	• Client numbers • Client (cross-border) numbers	• Satisfaction • Benefit delivered
Business development	• Pitch success	• Source of business
Standards	• Observance of standards	• Use of corporate databases
Thought leadership	• Publications • Media coverage	• Event attendance

Early in its journey to become a fully integrated cross-border operation, CBRE realised that a cohesive and coherent brand strategy would be an essential pillar, both to embolden internal staff, and to present a coherent face to outside organisations.

Being global meant that the firm's name would be associated with certain principles, regardless of where and how its customer base encountered the brand in action. If CBRE was seen as a different type of animal in Alabama, Albania and Auckland, globalisation could become counterproductive; an unwelcome experience in one location could taint the brand on the other side of the planet. CBRE settled on the theme of *going beyond*, meaning – as described in its brand guidelines – that "we do more, try harder, think deeper ... through our restlessness to do better and beat expectations every day." Through relentless and imaginative internal communications, affinity with the going beyond concept is nurtured across the 37,000-strong workforce. "Every person acts as an ambassador for the brand every time they interact with clients or colleagues," says Rhodes. "If they're not displaying the going beyond idea, it won't happen."

Developing his theme, Rhodes explains why *going beyond* is such a powerful essence for the CBRE brand. "Many attributes can be country specific and hard to export. For example, professional integrity can be a powerful differentiator in the United States. But in Europe, where the Royal Institution of Chartered Surveyors is so strong, it can be a generic characteristic of the entire category. So we wanted to differentiate ourselves on attitude." In addition to having a basis in reality ("that always helps!"), *going beyond* is sufficiently flexible that local teams have latitude and freedom to express it in different ways. Rhodes parades some examples: "Some can use it to show

how we push aggressively to get the best outcome for our clients. Others can use it to demonstrate our ability to think creatively and innovatively about the configuration of a new shopping centre. Others will use it to describe the way we mobilise teams with multilingual ability and diverse technical knowledge to value complex portfolios that are oceans apart."

CBRE's journey to global stature as a professional services firm remains incomplete. It has but a fraction of the scale of the big four accountancy practices such as *PricewaterhouseCoopers* and *KPMG*. In many markets, especially ones where it has recently entered, awareness of the firm is shallow and confined to born-and-bred property obsessives. In 2012, it published a brand building toolkit, *17 Ways To Build Your Brand*, for local teams to implement, replete with hints, tips, and headlines born of successes elsewhere. Each tool – hosting events, using signage, thinking digitally, publishing information – was crafted to raise consciousness within the market that CBRE is a firm that has things to say, and is unafraid to say them. For example, the item 'Get to Know Opinion Leaders' encourages readers to "regularly meet key real estate journalists, participate in trade events, participate in professional events." Through ingraining the going beyond attitude in the corporate cerebellum, it will – anticipates Rhodes – influence every facet of how the organisation represents itself, from the manner in which visitors are greeted in reception lobbies to how quarterly analyst updates are delivered.

Managing a global people business represents an extreme example of multi-faceted complexity. Unlike machinery, human beings can sulk, undermine, and depart. When that happens thousands of miles from head office, senior managers have a problem. CBRE's concentration on a careful programme of acquisitions, management structures that fuse local accountability with cross-border best practice, and global brand values designed for local expression have enabled it, so far, to survive the quagmire and race clear of the chasing pack.

RESPONSIVE TO COMMUNITIES AND CULTURES

Zurich Global Life is a provider of investment and protection solutions for high net worth individuals, and has seen almost every building block of its business model turned inside out by globalisation. Its investment activity must seek the best returns regardless of jurisdiction and landmass. Its executives spend much of their time managing the challenges associated with international timezones and markets at different stages of evolution. And, of course, many of its customers are internationally mobile. It's not uncommon for a Zurich policyholder to make the initial purchase in one country, transmit regular payments while working in a second, receive the maturity while domiciled in a third, and wish to remit funds to an extended family residing in a fourth. Mobility can be west to east or, increasingly, east to west, with the rules on tax and transfers constantly evolving at both home and destination.

With so many factors in play, Zurich's international propositions team felt the need to achieve a deeper insight into the attitudes, behaviours and future plans of different segments of its customer base. What is it that motivates a particular cohort to leave behind the country of their birth and education, and take up residency half way around the world? How do lifestyles differ for expatriates and international nomads compared with those who resist the temptation to set sail? Are there distinctive ways in which each group regards the accumulation of financial assets and the planning for retirement? And how might the answers to such questions inform the features and delivery of products bought to market by a brand such as Zurich?

Zurich's challenges were exacerbated by the highly segmented nature of the people that purchase its policies – whether in terms of gender, country of origin, age, marital status, disposable income, ethnicity, occupation, net worth, or relationship with their financial adviser. Zurich's Head of Insight, Simon Carpenter, summarises the issue: "We needed a better understanding of customers than was provided by a simplistic Net Promotor Score. That may have a place, but as part of a wider story. We needed to dive deep into the customer life journey. And by that, I don't just mean cradle to grave. It's also inter-generational, it's about parental advocacy. We needed to deploy techniques that would reveal answers on a whole different scale."

To further its understanding of the values, assumptions and circumstances that lie behind financial decisions, Zurich created a multi-year programme under the soubriquet Zurich Community, and commissioned research experts, *Merlin Communications*, to provide intellectual, technical and logistical support. The programme assembled a selection of individuals that either held Zurich plans, or had purchased in the past, or were actively considering options for the future. For example, in Hong Kong, the Community comprised (amongst others) an unmarried Australian lady, who had arrived in Kowloon shortly after the 1997 transfer of sovereignty, to freelance as a fashion designer; a former policeman from Birmingham, married with two grown-up children, who worked in education; a twenty-something team manager in a struggling boutique travel agency; and a Belgian entrepreneur who split his time between running a fast-growing factory in the Guangdong province and serving on the boards of half a dozen businesses run by friends and contacts.

Having assembled this motley crew, Zurich – at the outset – used focus groups to test and probe key issues. However, like adding a dash or two of tabasco sauce with a slice of chilli pepper to a bulldog gin, these were focus groups with a difference. Conventionally, focus groups gather one windswept evening for two hours of roving discussion, while cameras whirr and observers transcribe their notes, huddled on the far side of a one-way mirror; then, the participants depart the scene. Zurich felt this wasn't just looking a gift horse in the mouth, but repackaging the gift horse and lowering it on to a slow train to Siberia. Cavalier eviction of the respondents after the first conversation meant that opportunities to assess and track changes in their outlook over time were sadly foregone.

By contrast, the Zurich Community programme required the focus group moderator to build a relationship with the same group of respondents over a number of cycles. The ways in which individuals reflected on topics, and often changed their opinions, could be placed under a microscope. The evolution, from meeting to meeting, in how participants interacted with one another provided much material for contemplation. Of great interest were the thought processes through which those at various life stages assimilated product information (messages, features, statistics, case studies), digested it, and formed their conclusions. Carpenter observes, "The data was becoming so potentially rich and valuable that we needed to set up a steering group to determine the priority issues. Otherwise we risked receiving huge feedback on secondary points, or matters outside our control."

A tangible early result of the Community programme was the introduction of Flash Payments. It emerged from respondents that, when a crisis occurs, individuals often require urgent access to cash, and the need is exacerbated when it involves expatriates. Zurich introduced a "no-questions-asked" payment of up to ten per cent of the overall payout upon occurrence of such an event. In addition to the direct value for beneficiaries, this measure helped counter generic perceptions that insurers en bloc are delighted to receive premia and loathe to settle claims.

In recent years, the Zurich Community programme has evolved beyond its focus group origins. "We have made it scalable," says Carpenter. "The community has migrated online. We have recruited in the hundreds, and subjected respondents to stricter pre-screening. There are also certain rules of engagement to which they must adhere. Then we let them loose. It's been extraordinary to watch them engage unprompted with one another. From time to time, we lob in our prompts, and watch in fascination as the discussion evolves."

The flow of insight has allowed the Zurich team to forge products that are specifically designed to solve underlying concerns rather than superficial expressions of angst, and to communicate the benefits in ways that users and potential users find engaging and relatable. *Figure 2.4* reproduces one early output: a model created by Community participants themselves to reflect key life events, which was used as the basis for subsequent discussions on financial needs and planning.

FIGURE 2.4: Early Zurich Community output

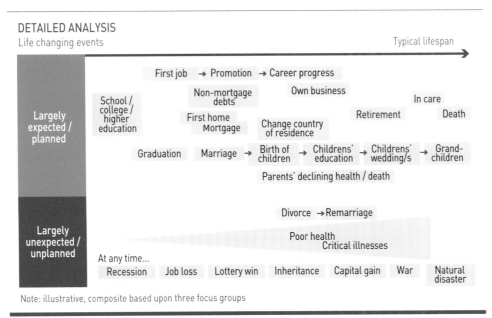

DETAILED ANALYSIS
Life changing events   Typical lifespan

Largely expected / planned

First job → Promotion → Career progress

School / college / higher education

Non-mortgage debts

First home Mortgage

Own business

Change country of residence

Retirement

In care

Death

Graduation   Marriage →   Birth of children →   Childrens' education →   Childrens' wedding/s →   Grand-children

Parents' declining health / death

Largely unexpected / unplanned

Divorce →Remarriage

Poor health
Critical illnesses

At any time...

Recession   Job loss   Lottery win   Inheritance   Capital gain   War   Natural disaster

Note: illustrative, composite based upon three focus groups

Source: Zurich Community

Among native Hong Kongers, the Zurich Community programme reinforced that life insurance and related products are supportive of, and compatible with, the role of filial piety (respect for parents) in Confucian philosophy. It revealed the nagging, perennial worries amongst the middle-aged that they cannot do more to support their parents. They saw the demands of work, commuting and modern life as sometimes at loggerheads with traditional values; the stool would only stay balanced with the three legs of money, time and health. It highlighted the changes from previous generations when large families were the norm, and security could reliably be provided by multiple family members. The declining birth rate posed a stark new challenge: should a high earner fall upon hard times, there may be insufficient resources even among the wider family to contribute what is needed. "We were amazed at the strength of culture as a segment descriptor," says Carpenter. "More so than age or gender or income. Retired Chinese share many of the same values as Chinese teenagers because of their common culture. We needed to develop our product design to respond to this profound point."

Turning to expatriates, the Zurich Community programme highlighted possible changes to policy conditions that would enhance appeal and relevance to those uncertain of their future residency, including rules around flexibility, currency and redemption. It also illuminated that this cohort had a different perspective on international risk.

On the one hand, they were by instinct global in their outlook and disposition. They felt confident and relaxed discussing the grand sweep of geopolitical events to a degree which might unnerve those to whom such matters are literally and metaphorically a foreign land. They displayed no emotional yearning for the bulk of their investments to be concentrated in sectors and locations for which they had feelings of nostalgia. On the other hand, those with a visa to work in Hong Kong for a defined period often argued that their personal risk exposure to the eastward march of the earth's centre of financial gravity was nearing its limits. Their home life and career were dependent upon the continued prosperity of the Asia Pacific region, and perhaps that was enough. Counter intuitively, it emerged, those with the deepest first-hand ties to emerging markets can exhibit a certain reluctance and trepidation about placing similar bets with their retirement wealth. The further their personal journey has taken them, the stronger their urge to deploy financial assets in ways that maintain an anchor, however feeble its grip, back to their birthland.

Carpenter is adamant this wealth of insight isn't being generated to languish – admired but unloved – in a central dashboard. A growing proportion of his time is now invested in working with countries from South America to the Middle East and out towards the Pacific on making a difference to outcomes.

"I'm faintly obsessive about two outcomes above all," he argues. "Firstly, if the customers ask for something to be fixed, we must listen and respond. That's how we have increased our global protection sales in recent years, by applying new knowledge on a global basis. But more profoundly, we need to use this insight to continually transform our culture, so that every element of our processes and propositions are designed with the customer in mind."

Carpenter's message to his country colleagues is stark: if they sign up to the Zurich Community programme, he will commit to support their participation through sizeable central resources. But all is conditional upon evidence that the findings are being taken seriously. He is insistent everyone benefits when insights are transformed into action, and is unafraid to wield either carrot, or stick, or both simultaneously. "A global business won't stay that way if everyone is happy in silos. Zurich Community is one facet, among many, that's shattering silos beyond repair."

TRANSPORTATION, PROPERTY AND FINANCE. In many ways, they are highly divergent sectors, starkly different in the types of employee they attract, their brand ambitions, their uses of capital, their process intensity, their public reputation, their regulatory framework. Yet each has been at the heart of the globe's transformation, since the 1800s, from a series of largely self-contained commercial fiefdoms into one enormous bazaar.

Key players in these vital marketplaces may have employed a variety of strategies in pursuit of their worldwide ambitions: from bold, headline-grabbing acquisitions, to the establishment of low key liaison offices. But, in every case, globalisation will not succeed if it is pursued as a parcelled-up, arm's length project. It demands, fundamental, enterprise-wise changes to how business is conducted. A one-size-fits-all philosophy can be effective when applied single-mindedly to limited product lines, serving limited customer segments, in limited geographies. As soon as sights are raised beyond its immediate local borders, the firm's mindset – and, by extension, its entire business model – must enter a new phase. The qualities of flexibility, pragmatism and responsiveness move to the fore.

In this chapter, I have explored how exemplar firms have geared up organisationally to stamp a prodigious international footprint; how they have stimulated the sharing of knowledge and insight throughout the network; and how they have ensured customer-facing activities are sensitive to the nuances and expectations of communities and cultures. To last the distance, the global business cannot choose at leisure between these qualities, as if they are coloured candies in a pick-and-mix. A thriving global business must embrace every one.

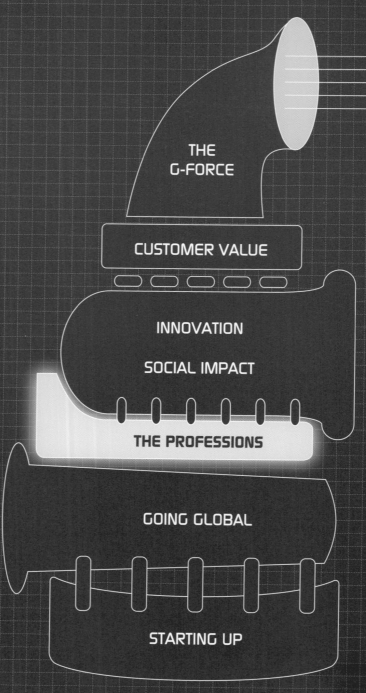

THE
G-FORCE

CUSTOMER VALUE

INNOVATION

SOCIAL IMPACT

THE PROFESSIONS

GOING GLOBAL

STARTING UP

FACING AN AGE OF CYNICISM

- Many consumers see professionals as often self-interested
- Professionals can no longer claim exclusive access to hidden knowledge
- Many employers have scaled back their investment in professionalism.

STAYING CURRENT THEN STEPPING AHEAD
(ROYAL INSTITUTION OF CHARTERED SURVEYORS)

- Professional careers are more diverse, but less linear
- Without lifelong learning, entry level professional knowledge is quickly outdated
- Far-sighted professionals re-equip themselves for tomorrow's challenges.

IN TEAMS AND IN EMPLOYMENT
(CHARTERED INSTITUTE OF PURCHASING AND SUPPLY,
CHARTERED INSTITUTE OF MARKETING)

- Teams, not just individuals, can be measured against objective professional benchmarks
- Professionals are under pressure to demonstrate the Return On Investment (ROI) of their trade
- Employers expect professional insight to pinpoint new opportunities.

APPLYING KNOWLEDGE
(ASSOCIATION OF CHARTERED CERTIFIED ACCOUNTANTS)

- In addition to knowledge, complete professionalism demands ethical behaviour and skills in strategic analysis, interpersonal relationships
- Professional judgement is an essential complement to process compliance
- Professionals must act as facilitators, applying knowledge to assess options.

CHARTERED STATUS AND THE PUBLIC INTEREST
(PROFESSIONAL ASSOCIATION RESEARCH NETWORK,
CHARTERED INSURANCE INSTITUTE)

- Professional bodies have sparked widespread discussion about public interest benefits and the measurement of impact
- The Chartered concept is respected internationally as a symbol of standards
- The bar must be raised if the Chartered badge is to continue embodying the pinnacle of professionalism.

"LAWYERS LEAVE YOU penniless then doctors finish you off."

With sentiments such as these, expressed during a recent *Chase Noble* focus group on professionalism, now widespread, it seems a line has been drawn under the age of deference. In fact, a line does scant justice to the extent of the demarcation. The age of deference has been gutted, chained, wrapped in seven shrouds, buried on the far side of the chasm, and the last remaining rope bridge has been torched. It will not return in a hurry.

The small town bank manager who knew his customers by name and would extend an overdraft, no questions asked, to the builder unable to meet the month's payroll. The local GP dropping in to check the wellbeing of her elderly patients while walking home from the clinic. The policeman having a word with young ruffians caught stealing apples. The journalist filing puff pieces about the school fete with nary a word sourced via phone hacking. These stereotypes were once not without foundation. The professions used to enjoy elevated status within communities. They were trusted, revered, esteemed; their pedestals untarnished.

FACING AN AGE OF CYNICISM

The Chase Noble focus groups took place across the country, and included sessions in London, Glasgow, Bristol, Birmingham and Manchester. Participants were taken from a cross-section of society, reflecting the local demographics in terms of gender, age, occupation and ethnicity. The message was forceful: the incessant demystification of the professions over recent years has taken its toll. The banking crisis, the investigation into abnormal death rates at Mid Staffordshire Hospital, the arrest and prosecution of newspaper editors and journalists, and the scandal over MP expenses which led *in extremis* to custodial sentences, have not gone unnoticed.

One focus group participant, the owner of a small London-based design business, expressed it thus: "Elitism doesn't mean anything. It certainly doesn't mean they are more attentive. Too many of the so-called professions operate like a closed shop. Self-preservation trumps all." Another commented dismissively: "You can buy your way into anything." And a third, a working mother in Bristol, was sceptical about the nature and content of suggestions she received from professional advisers, irrespective of their qualifications: "They are not so creative, they are too tied into a set way of doing things. They plan well, but always inside a box. They find it impossible to deviate from the rules, and can't deal with unusual situations." The words and phrases most frequently employed by respondents, including the most damning, are reproduced in *Figure 3.1*.

FIGURE 3.1: Unprompted associations with the concept of professionalism

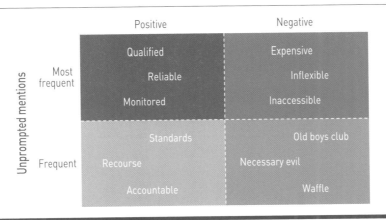

Source: Chase Noble focus groups of general public and SME owners

A further theme from the focus groups was that the commoditisation of information has profoundly affected the public mood. At a click or two, websites can be accessed on every conceivable topic, from the technical to the obscure, to the technically obscure. Knowledge is no longer a scare resource, hidden from wider view. Professionals have not acquired insights via some sublime alchemy that are impenetrable and beyond challenge.

On the contrary, sites from Wikipedia to Yahoo Answers now provide a synthesis of material that, two decades past, was not available beyond the confines of elite institutions. The facts sometimes get distorted, misconstrued or wrongly-defined, but they are no longer exclusively the prerogative of the blessed few. Amidst this maelstrom of evolving knowledge, educational practices are struggling to remain relevant. Is entry into a profession determined by the ability to recite a canon of knowledge? Clearly, this has a role, but is it sufficient?

One focus group, comprised of aspiring professionals from diverse sectors, concluded that years spent in rote memorisation of key data was now redundant. Facts can be checked within moments; moreover, information can change so quickly – amended through legislation, different guidance, an updated evidence base – that relying purely on recollection veers towards negligence. On the other hand, there's no short cut to competence in listening, analysing, interpreting and especially applying knowledge. The dictum of philosopher, John Dewey, that "we can have facts without thinking, but we cannot have thinking without facts" may need to be recalibrated for the modern era.

The Manchester focus group involved business leaders rather than young professionals or the users of professional services. Eight managing directors agreed the uncertain economic outlook was forcing them to be more frugal and less cavalier in funding the professional development of staff on an open-ended basis. They ask whether they can justify intense investment in upskilling their workforce when the next round of redundancies is just around the corner. They struggle to justify training budgets whose payback, if any, comes over the long term, when the boardroom preoccupation may be survival to the year end. As the corporate meat cleaver hacks away at spend of dubious value, they see the payment of professional body subscriptions on behalf of employees as a relatively easy and pain-free target for cutting. This poses a challenge; one which professionals across the board are needing to meet with diligence, imagination and a dash of chutzpah.

STAYING CURRENT THEN STEPPING AHEAD

Before our eyes, society is metamorphosing too rapidly for the traditional concept of the professional to survive. Obtaining a prestigious qualification no longer bestows the right to trade off the certificate through to retirement.

Medical breakthroughs make the favoured treatments of yesterday redundant. The publishers of *Tolley's Tax Guide* could never contemplate reprinting editions, verbatim and without revision, from one year to the next. Data from empirical studies into recruitment, selection, motivation, retention and remuneration are continually reshaping the ways human resource professionals undertake their roles. Information technology professionals could not possibly ply their craft if their competence had been frozen in the era of the Olivetti P6060, weighing in at 40 kilograms and complete with its 32 character plasma display, 48 kilobytes of RAM and eight inch external floppy disk drive. And financial advisers find the products that once topped the performance tables, are now liable to land them with a compensation claim.

The breakneck pace at which accepted best practice becomes antiquated and tarnished means that constant re-acquaintance with basic tenets and knowledge is now the hallmark of professionalism. Accomplishments decades past at one's alma mater are good foundations, but no more.

Sean Tompkins, chief executive of the *Royal Institution of Chartered Surveyors* (RICS), argues with passion that maintaining competence is integral to the concept of professionalism. "The professions are under the public spotlight as never before. External users want to know that professionals are maintaining standards. They see the professional body as giving the assurance their members are bang up to date. This is the heart of the public interest test."

Surveying is one of the disciplines where breakneck advances have occurred affecting both theory and practice. Commercial property valuers, whose role once simply involved assembling comparables and calculating yields, have started incorporating a raft of new variables into their assessments, such as construction materials, energy efficiency, accessibility for transportation purposes, and accreditation from one of the green building certification agencies. These factors have prompted RICS to refocus its efforts from the entry level qualification (which of course remains), to Continuing Professional Development (CPD).

Tompkins remarks: "Over the past few years we have overhauled the CPD arrangements, for example for valuers. Our Valuer Registration Programme requires every valuer to commit to CPD that is relevant for their role, including any specialisms they carry. There are so many examples where a surveyor's level of competence cannot be guaranteed by an exam sat decades ago. For example, a bigger element of the work is around dispute resolution, arbitration and expert witness. Members must have the tools for those types of tasks." Another example he offers is the shift in investors' priorities towards managing lifetime value. "Surveyors must be able to look at future use, or the upgrading of buildings that once seemed grand but are no longer desirable, or marketing to global tenants."

Many partners in surveying practices entered a cottage profession in the 20th century, marked by national idioms and characteristics, starting from such basic matters as how to define the footprint of a building, and whether to use metric or imperial measurements. Local practices are hard to reconcile, argues Tompkins, with an age when pension fund managers are investing in property globally, and need a common understanding of the assets within their portfolios. "Global capital movements mean common standards are not a luxury, they are vital. For decades, properties have been valued in different ways from country to country. Do you count car parking space in the footprint? Reception areas? Roof terraces? With American banks lending in southern Europe, and French banks lending in Africa, and Asian banks lending in the Middle East, you need clarity of international practice." Pressure for this to ascend the RICS priority list has even come from intergovernmental sources: "We are working with the World Bank to define essentials that are globally applicable, and working for example in Brazil, China and India – where we have been involved in launching a university joint venture – to bring them into reality."

But staying current is insufficient; the complete professional needs to discern trends that will emerge and dominate during the times ahead. In a single year, RICS has published materials on topics as diverse as the impact of climate change on building operating costs through to 2100, the long-term regeneration strategy unveiled by the Scottish government, and the anticipated shortage of 44 million construction professionals by 2020 in India alone. Entry to the professions must see young talent equipped with the tools to future-proof their skills; the confidence to absorb and deploy insights which lie beyond the horizon. Devising tests that tease out these traits, and applying them fearlessly and fairly, will stretch educational assessment practice, but is unavoidable in a fast-paced sector.

Contributing to the renaissance of the profession now sits alongside knowledge and ethics as a mark of a well-rounded practitioner. Many professional bodies have seen an upsurge in the willingness of members to put something back, for example through mentoring, lecturing, assisting with syllabi reviews, participating in peer review, or inputting into policy documents. In a typical year, RICS may publish around 42 technical guides on everything from asbestos handling to Japanese knotweed to conflicts of interest. These cannot be perfected if authors are left to draft and edit in isolation. Relevant, leading edge content is dependent on practitioners giving voluntarily of their time to make suggestions, contribute data and review.

With many issues of technical knowledge and commercial application subject to convulsion and flux, new entrants to the professions are less clear than their forebears about the likely career journey ahead. Simplistic notions that one acquires the all-important letters in one's mid-20s, and then looks forward to 35 years of gradually advancing status and remuneration, are outdated. Today's young professionals do not anticipate a predictable linear career progression. "I haven't thought beyond the next few years," said a newly-qualified 23-year-old leasing agent in one focus group. "I'm taking my life in five year chunks." Sabbaticals, career switches and re-education into related specialties are becoming the new normal. "It's not an option to wait decades in the faint hope that one day I'll fill dead men's shoes," added a colleague.

RICS has also recognised this phenomenon. "The route to joining the profession has significantly widened," observes Tompkins. "Historically most surveyors had an accredited surveying degree. Now you see law degrees and business degrees and second degrees. And this unpredictability carries through. It's not unusual for professionals to move from private practice into a bank and back, or perhaps they fancy broadening their experience for a time with a landlord or a fund. This is an important boundary change." Property, argues Tompkins, is now seen as an asset class not just bricks and mortar. "So surveyors who stay current in their knowledge, and are able to apply this commercially, can use their background and insight in many different ways."

IN TEAMS AND IN EMPLOYMENT

Professional bodies trace their origins back to the medieval guilds, whereby artisans practicing a particular trade within a town would organise or associate in an agreed manner. In these early days, the aim of the guilds was unashamedly, even explicitly, forged in blatant self-interest. Fraternities of workers, perhaps in textiles or masonry or stonecutting or glassmaking, would commit – often through oath – to support one another in adversity, and to protect the mysteries of their craft. Over time, the guilds were granted certain privileges by the authorities, for example to indirectly limit competition through the control and restriction of apprenticeships.

Over the centuries, professional bodies accrued a number of more high-minded goals, or at least adopted more amenable phrasing to express their self-interest. The setting of entry standards through examination became a core responsibility, necessitating the preparation of syllabi, the publication of learning materials and the awarding of technical qualifications. Parallel functions often included the promotion of some type of ethical code, the disciplining or expulsion of malingerers, and the organisation of social events, networking evenings and ceremonial occasions. During much of the post-war period, their place remained in the background: part of society's complex infrastructure, generally under-appreciated, but with a role that was rarely questioned in terms of fundamental principles.

The role of these bodies needs to change if they are to prosper during the 21st century. One factor is the importance of corporate employers, rather than individual members, to their strategies and product range. For example, for many years, the *Chartered Institute of Purchasing and Supply* (CIPS) has been acutely sensitive to the needs of c-suite leaders. Among the many challenges is the tendency of harried chief executives to express impatient frustration with specialist functional disciplines that lie beyond the boundaries of their personal expertise. When making unpalatable budget decisions, how can they be reassured such departments are operating to a satisfactory standard? In straightened times, they no longer have the luxury of accepting bland assertions from in-post executives in defence of their patch. Few firms have sufficiently bountiful cash flow to grant the benefit of the doubt to every glad-handing departmental head. How can leaders in such circumstances be satisfied their procurement functions meet acceptable, objective standards?

"I came from that world," explains chief executive David Noble. "Professional bodies used to offer a one size fits all approach. That role is gone, we're facing a revolution." Noble saw CIPS' relevance to the corporate sector being rooted, above all, in its ability to articulate the shape and scale of the benchmark. "Then we can tell them where they sit on the continuum. Are they world class? And we recently made the first platinum award to the Royal Mail procurement team. Or are they on the journey? And, if so, what needs to be put in place to close the gap?"

The assessment, or certification, of procurement teams involves a number of components, in particular people, processes and performance. CIPS's conviction is that a rounded function must be able to integrate and harmonise these elements; none can be prioritised at the expense of the others. Effective supply chain solutions – meaning ones that are lasting, do not create risk exposure and command public confidence – require competent individuals to work together, delivering measurable results within an appropriate framework. *Figure 3.2* depicts how an initial health check can lead to an assessment according to five core dimensions, and then an outcome assessment with platinum status at the summit.

FIGURE 3:2: CIPS corporate certification pathway

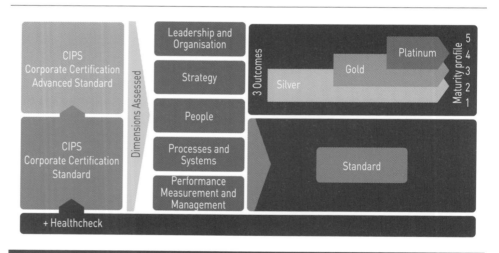

Source: Chartered Institute of Purchasing and Supply

"Benchmarking is not about a tick box template," adds CIPS Marketing Director Catherine Hill. "For example, when we look at how people gain knowledge, there are so many options. College, night school, self-study using books, self-study using e-learning, a five-day modular programme in a hotel. And now other tools we've developed that combine in-house training and project work, so employers get a benefit today from the work being done by individuals to progress to our MCIPS qualification." According to the CIPS model, benchmarking involves understanding the unique characteristics of individual situations, coupled with the exercise of discretion, rather than enforcing adherence to a predetermined checklist.

Neither is the benchmark standard an absolute, static for all time. Noble argues that the practice of supply chain management is being transformed due to external pressures including globalisation, the growing complexity of business relationship networks, and governance processes within the public sector and major firms. "How do professionals deal with tier three and four in the supply chain to stop the next horsemeat-type scandal? How do they influence ongoing contract management, not simply the initial award? How do category management techniques vary? How should global procurement hubs, such as Barclays' in Singapore, be operated? And where is there a burning platform that means the risk of fraud, supplier failure and one-sided contracts can only be eliminated by an effective licence to practice for the Chief Procurement Officer?" Most of these issues, says Noble, were not on the horizon a few years ago. "Now, they are imminent and pressing."

With the commercial landscape in upheaval, CIPS sees the measure of great procurement undergoing a fundamental reappraisal. Procurement professionals who diligently adhere to yesterday's standards will be woefully ill-equipped for the coming tsunami of challenges. This belief recently led CIPS to set out a series of provocative forecasts for the next two decades, in its highly influential report *An 80/20 vision*, which concluded that by 2032 – the year of CIPS' centenary – both the institute and its members would "look very different". The core skills of analysis and negotiation would, of necessity, be supplemented by a requirement to be respected, persuasive, visionary, strategic, sharp, global, collaborative, executive and business savvy. For these reasons, for Hill, benchmarking always returns to the calibre of the professional. "Operating as a functional person, and being part of the leadership team, are very different roles," she concludes. "Simply being better at procurement won't get someone their next job. If your only style is tough negotiating, you won't be a valued colleague at the top table. At that level, you make your impact through influence, not force."

The *Chartered Institute of Marketing* (CIM) has been equally concerned with the role of professionalism in the workplace. Chief Executive, Anne Godfrey, sees this redefining the heart of what it means to be a professional body, and by extension to be a professional. She explains: "Most of us have a model that hasn't changed for decades. Learning content used to come exclusively from professional bodies, now it's from publishing companies and online subscription businesses. If people need a template for a marketing plan, they use Google to search; they don't call us. The proposition we offer our members must be updated for the 21st century, end of story."

For Godfrey, Return On Investment (ROI) has moved from the periphery to the heart of the Institute's purpose. In an era when line item expenditure in corporate accounts is scrutinised internally and externally with microscopic ferocity, professionals are under unprecedented pressure to demonstrate their worth. "ROI is now all over our study offer. The core of our programmes is not marketing theory, or how to stay out of jail by following the law. It's giving marketers the skills and tools to make themselves, and their employers, more successful."

The focus on ROI has been key to once again aligning the interests of the individual members of the CIM with the corporate employers paying their wages. "Firms want more for less, and marketers want to keep busy. In the past, even the top marketing directors, churning out award-winning campaigns, have been ill-equipped to communicate internally." A pressing need is often to promote marketing to the board as more than colouring in. "They need to show the CEO that marketing directly impacts growth and share price. And to the Finance Director, how it affects the bottom line. And to other colleagues, such as Human Resources or Procurement, how Marketing has positive repercussions in those areas. Whether or not the Marketing Director sits on the board is secondary. The priority is that the board – the entire board – appreciates its value."

When the current suspicious mindset is shown to be commercially detrimental in comparison with more overt and activist support for the professional agenda, cautious chief executives will consider taking the next step – such as releasing individuals to serve their profession through volunteering to run special interest groups for their institute, fulfilling strenuous CPD obligations, or engaging in pro bono work.

APPLYING KNOWLEDGE

The maturing relationship of professional to canon of knowledge is perhaps most clearly seen in the world of high finance. Neil Stevenson, Executive Director of Brand at the *Association of Chartered Certified Accountants* (ACCA), argues that the accountant's role today is far removed from the historic 'bean counting' caricature. "It was already changing, but more so since the financial crisis. With less money, less certainty and more volatility, investors and boards are desperate to understand the value drivers."

Stevenson supports his case by reference to the newly strategic involvement of many accountants, helping resources to be deployed effectively. "The British government is increasingly valuing finance experts at the heart of each department to instil better financial management disciplines." For him, far-sighted organisations no longer conceive of the state of their ledger in splendid isolation from everything else that's occurring. "Integrated reporting is key. In future, performance will not be disclosed through a series of disconnected documents, like the profit and loss (P&L) and the corporate and social responsibility (CSR) report. The professional accountant will drive a more rounded view of how the organisation is using financial capital, manufacturing capital, human capital, intellectual capital and brand capital to create long-term value."

The ACCA's vision for the future of its profession is causing Richter scale shockwaves in the ways that aspiring accountants are recruited, trained and assessed. Technical ability cannot, of course, be dismissed; but it now sits within a broader competency framework. "We now focus on ten areas, of which one is corporate reporting," explains Stevenson. "The others include stakeholder management, strategy, ethics alongside core areas of accounting. Anyone entering the profession as a trainee must start developing all these skills, through a combination of experience or study." He ticks off the career options that may lie ahead, perhaps as business leaders, practitioners, entrepreneurs, non-executives. "They will need a rounded skill set to succeed in any of these roles."

The competency framework, which is summarised in *Figure 3.3*, underpins ACCA's contention that the complete professional must be able to operate using a multitude of styles to be effective. Depending on the occasion, they may be called upon to challenge, influence, argue, explain, rationalise, illustrate, deconstruct or forecast. Individuals holding a cupboard full of A starred certificates, but who lack the behavioural intelligence to function in awkward or unpredictable circumstances, will be unable to fulfil their professional obligations. They will find themselves wailing pitifully from the sidelines, like an ineffective football coach whose team is chasing shadows, on the verge of cup elimination.

FIGURE 3.3: ACCA competency framework for the complete finance professional
Percentage of Chief Financial Officers deeming each competence essential for newly qualified professionals

Competence	Scope (not comprehensive)	%
Financial management	Investment appraisal, business reorganisation, risk management, treasury, working capital	96%
Professionalism and ethics	Ethical behaviour, personal ethics, corporate ethical framework	94%
Corporate reporting	Business reports to support understanding and decision-making	93%
Sustainable management accounting	Business performance planning, measuring, controlling, monitoring, value creation	87%
Governance, risk and control	Risk identification procedures, internal audit and control systems	86%
Strategy and innovation	Options to improve performance and position, change management, business process improvement	86%
Leadership and management	Effective and ethical organisational leadership, resource management, understanding stakeholders	83%
Audit and assurance	High quality external audits, evaluating information systems and controls, gathering evidence	80%
Law and taxation	Understanding legislation and regulations, establishing tax liabilities, tax planning	78%
Stakeholder relationship management	Engaging stakeholders effectively, communicating relevant information	68%

Source: ACCA

In this newly emerging world, the role of the professional is not simply to place a conclusion before the masses, and then depart the scene. Professionals are increasingly required to help their clients assess options and decide the appropriate course. Medical practitioners no longer conceal a distressing diagnosis from ailing patients; they will be open about the prospects, however harrowing, and work with the sufferer and the wider family on choices to mitigate the situation. "We call this the professional as change maker," says Stevenson. "Using judgement not following checklists. Applying their knowledge ethically and responsibly, not always enforcing prescribed rules."

In future, should the ACCA's vision prevail, the rounded finance professional will spend more time applying knowledge to inform strategic decisions, than retrospectively reconciling cash in and out. With much of the developed world having endured a half-decade of minimal economic growth, governments, public companies and the third sector are facing tough choices on sharing a sometimes shrinking pie between more plates. The accountant can help decision-making to reach conclusions that are fully cognisant of the panoply of possible consequences, from the balance sheet to the risk register. And not just decisions that fall squarely in the chief financial officer's lap (tax mitigation, dividend cover), but broader questions such as the type of acquisitions, the balance between insourcing and supply chain leverage, or the pace of retrenchment. This is the chief financial officer - not as the semi-detached boffin hunched in the corner - but as expert witness, facilitator and guide.

CHARTERED STATUS AND THE PUBLIC INTEREST

Let us return for a moment to the recent consumer focus groups. Whilst probing the views of a sceptical public, some nuances emerged. The professions are indeed regarded with suspicion, but respondents felt the harshest generalisations were unwarranted and too indiscriminate. They recognise that tiers exist, and those who excel are a class apart.

In particular, the concept of *Chartered* still carries caché. Respondents felt it symbolised a commitment to go beyond basic, satisfier standards. "It says to me they've put in a lot of effort," said a young restaurateur. "There's been a more rigorous seal of approval, ultimately it comes from the Crown," added a project manager.

When the soubriquet *Chartered* appears on business cards or office doors, the public seem to take a degree of reassurance. The focus group delved at some length into the origins of this comfort and fortitude, and uncovered two assumptions. People assumed that a Chartered service would be more costly, but that it would likely offer better value: "The cost of a Chartered surveyor will probably be double your bog-standard surveyor," said an advertising agency receptionist. "But, it's the top slice of the pyramid. If a Chartered surveyor advised me on installing a steel beam, I'll be a lot more confident the house won't collapse," she added. Respondents also asserted that, should something go awry, with Chartered professionals the process of redress and restitution will be smoother and speedier. "Chartered financial planners don't need to wear pinstripes; flip-flops and shorts are fine," said a Birmingham headmaster. "Because if they're Chartered, and I lose out, they will deal with me fairly and the professional indemnity will pay up," he added.

Andy Friedman, Chief Executive Officer of the *Professional Associations Research Network* (PARN), which undertakes research on behalf of professional bodies, is effusive about the Chartered badge, and highlights the rapid increase in the number of associations and institutes seeking approval from the Privy Council to convert their status to that of a Chartered body. "Its international profile is extraordinarily positive," he comments. "Outside the Americas, which do plough their own way, it's seen as hugely prestigious. Whether in China, India, the Middle East, Australia and Africa, I've seen UK professional bodies make great strides because Chartered is seen as distinctive and – in a good way – elitist."

In modern Britain, elitism is often stigmatised by desperate politicians in search of easy applause on talk shows and panels. But many other cultures maintain the uncluttered conviction that educational excellence is both a virtue in itself and of wider social benefit. It's little wonder those countries where elitism is not only free from pejorative class overtones, but is embraced and celebrated, face the coming decades with optimism and confidence. They have seized the principles of achieving Chartered status, and encouraged its evolution from a quirky oddity of the constitution in a small island off Europe's north west coastline into an archetype with global resonance.

International yearning for a Chartered title is one of the many factors that have led professional bodies to redefine themselves on a stage that stretches beyond narrow national borders. Members' careers are more likely to include secondments to hot spots thousands of miles from London's coffee shops. Corporations may see the UK as a shrinking, scarcely visible footnote to their global operations. And overseas governments and regulators, when introducing a new institutional framework or licence to practice, often approach UK practitioners for counsel. However, this isn't quite the endorsement of British competence it might, at first blush, appear; since industrialisation had its origins in Derbyshire mills, overseas policymakers are often seeking to understand the errors and mis-steps that have littered Britain's story for the past 200 years, in order to avoid repeating the same mistakes.

There is no consistent model being grasped by professional bodies as they adapt in the face of international opportunities. Some are deliberately, consciously constructing a unified worldwide Chartered body, often in response to parallel moves to harmonise regulations from one jurisdiction to the next. Complex mergers using supra-national Swiss Verein structures have been used to overcome local resistance and the perception of belligerent land-grabs. Other bodies have adopted a different stance, and aim to affiliate with or otherwise support in-country bodies, supplying content without expecting control. This has been referred to as the equivalent, in the professionalism arena, to the legendary *Intel inside* strategy pursued by the world's largest semiconductor chip manufacturer. Others seek simply to share experiences and nurture local professionalism before moving on – delivering a public benefit on the largest possible canvass, albeit with little direct benefit to domestic members, and running the risk that motives may be misconstrued.

Still other bodies are opportunistic, assessing every option against tough business case criteria, and only proceeding when they see the prospect of a commercial dividend that can benefit their longest-standing stakeholders. And finally there is the risk mitigation model, wherein a proportion of sales to non-domestic end users is counted a virtue in itself. Irrespective of the locations chosen, or profit margins achieved, to these strategists overseas revenue streams imply a more balanced, hence resilient, business model. Each of these five approaches has merit and can gain traction; the bodies that have tended to struggle internationally are those which lack clarity of vision. Such organisations have defaulted to overseas expansion because it instinctively seems a good idea, and not as the outcome of an articulated purpose or objective.

Potentially the most significant, and exciting, application of Chartered principles on the global stage is occurring in Africa, described by Tony Blair as recently as 2001 as a "stain on the conscience of the world." ACCA's Stevenson remarks: "This is where our public value remit can be most dramatically discharged. Countries on the path of development need institutions that are free from fraud, business that is conducted with sound discipline, and a supply chain that can be transacted with confidence." Rich in natural resources, boasting the youngest demographic of any continent, enjoying GDP growth in excess of six per cent, with increasing signs of legitimate and open government in countries such as Botswana and Mauritius, and with the world's largest professional services firm, PwC, having recently announced a $100 million, three-year African investment programme in talent and infrastructure. It seems the continent may finally be poised to be a lead actor in the global theatre. Historic events such as Africa's awakening can be expedited when Chartered professionals are able to contribute as mentors, teachers and creators.

To protect the Chartered lustre, PARN's Friedman is adamant that the transition from an old-style club to a respected Chartered body confers responsibilities and duties. "The tie pins and cuff links and gold chains don't need to be thrown away. Nostalgia and heritage have a place. But we're strongly of the view that efficient and streamlined governance arrangements are a prerequisite if professional bodies are to fulfil a public interest role," he says. Large representative councils, sometimes numbering over a hundred, can be a legitimate tool according to PARN's prescriptions, but only if constituted alongside a smaller executive board. "And that board cannot only comprise eminent persons from the profession. Lay people must sit alongside, who can prod and cajole their colleagues to dispense with their insular preoccupations, and look to the wider picture."

For legacy reasons, many professional bodies are encumbered with articles of association written by founding fathers (almost always fathers) using quill pen, antiquated terminology, and a pinch of snuff. The original parchments make no reference to activity outside UK shores (or, if they do, only to expressly forbid it). The transition to Chartered status is often the catalyst for such documents to be retrieved from the chambers, dusted down, and reworked for the modern challenges. "I've seen some of these original memoranda that mandate the body does nothing more than maintain a library and make available meeting rooms," says Friedman. "If you listed the most important contributions for today, neither of those points would make the top 50."

Chartered bodies are able to bestow the title upon individuals and sometimes firms as a dispensation granted at the pleasure of the Privy Council. The criteria they apply often combine many of the factors this chapter has been discussing – qualifications, a commitment to continued professional competence and relevance, ethical behaviour, evidence of outstanding delivery over a substantial period, and a wider contribution to the development of the profession. The kernel is that Chartered goes far beyond basic reliability with a limited toolkit. It isn't about achieving minimum standards, it's about busting through the ceiling and still not stopping. *Figure 3.4* depicts how the Chartered Insurance Institute (CII) positions the Chartered designation in relation both to its broader suite of designations and to the equivalent educational level.

And through it runs one further variable, which is a belief that the interests of the immediate stakeholders – the professional himself or herself, their colleagues, their employers – are secondary and subservient to the public interest.

"There's a word that, I believe, summarises the Chartered ethos. And that word is *courage*," comments Friedman. "Courage to stick with your convictions, and to speak out, even if it puts your own interests at risk." Chartered bodies can offer irreplaceable support to professionals who may find themselves in a situation of potential compromise. They can hold out a safe haven, offer confidential counselling, and guide them through the tangle of options for turning whistle-blower. Their involvement can be more multi-faceted, practical and subtle than a professional might receive if they went directly to the authorities.

FIGURE 3.4: CII framework to the Chartered pinnacle

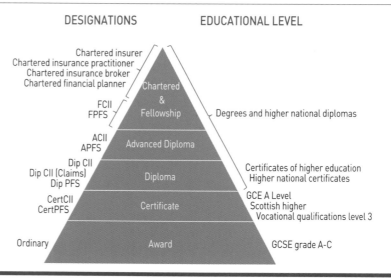

Source: Chartered Insurance Institute

Frenetic debate has been underway in the sector during recent years to bring greater clarity and definition to the concept of the public interest. A number of aspects, previously seen as secondary or tangential, have assumed greater weight, including how whistle-blowing is addressed, how ethical practices are embedded, a more activist approach to quality assurance and monitoring to stamp out underperformance, and more transparency when disciplinary measures or expulsions are enacted.

Frameworks for fulfilling a public interest purpose have been developed by, for example, Leeds University, the Professional Benchmarking Group, and PARN itself. At the heart of many schemes is the quest to assess Proof Of Impact. In many professions, the details are still elusive, and attempts to quantify a public good will often be bogged down either in the swamp of semi-political arguments (are all "members of the public" equal?), or the quagmire of philosophical speculations (we can only be certain about what happened, not what might have otherwise transpired), or the quicksand of satisfying empirical statistical thresholds. Emerging from this morass will be, many expect, consensus around Proof of Impact tests which assemble multiple variables, including the experiences of informed parties, the perceptions of control groups, and a suite of hard measures that vary by profession.

Awareness of the power of the Chartered brand has led many institutes to raise the bar to its attainment, sometimes gradually but often with alacrity. The CII, which launched a corporate Chartered title in 2007 with a limited number of criteria related primarily to qualifications, is currently revamping the standard to supplement the initial focus on Competence with facets of Conduct and Culture. References are now made (subject to the outcome of ongoing consultation) to the customer journey, client satisfaction, complaint handling, document transparency and supplier relationships. The tightening standards have resulted, in part, from an appreciation of the great store customers place by the Chartered message, and also by practitioners themselves arguing that Chartered must symbolise a more rounded set of capabilities than simply the passing of examinations. Underpinning the updated approach is a vision that explicitly references the end result of a professional's endeavours: "Being a Chartered firm brings with it a public interest responsibility, a responsibility to the wider Chartered brand, and a responsibility to the professional body."

Dr Sandy Scott, Chief Executive Officer at the CII, is determined the Chartered concept must retain its lustre. "Professional bodies that dumb down sow the seeds of their own destruction and irrelevance," he remarks in characteristically blunt terms. "We are heading in the opposite direction. For individuals, the Chartered designation cannot be achieved through qualifications alone. For corporates, we're actively raising the threshold, introducing new standards and making it harder to secure. That's the only way to ensure there's a public interest benefit which must, every time, supersede any commercial benefit to those that have obtained the badge."

IN THE FACE of the age of cynicism, professional bodies need to maintain confidence in the concept of professionalism and the status of the Chartered motif. If the professionals' pedestals are no longer as ubiquitous as soapboxes at Speaker's Corner, hopefully they're not yet extinct, or confined to museums alongside other historic curiosities. Custodians of the Chartered brand must resist short-term temptations or pressures to dilute. The label must embody in one simple descriptor the concepts of maintaining competence, looking ahead, applying knowledge, and fulfilling a public interest purpose. Following these precepts, the Chartered message may obtain a place without peer – as Rachmaninoff's third, or the Mona Lisa, or Ulysses, or the Hanging Gardens of Babylon. Akin to the *totalmente a mano* label on a box of handmade Cuban cigars; often mimicked, never matched.

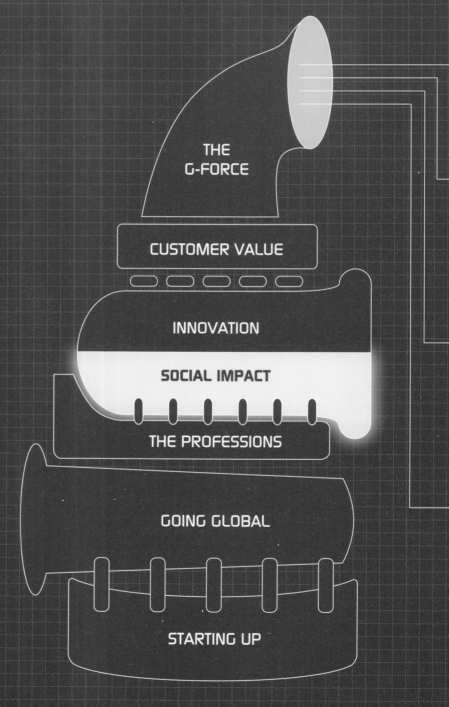

THE
G-FORCE

CUSTOMER VALUE

INNOVATION

SOCIAL IMPACT

THE PROFESSIONS

GOING GLOBAL

STARTING UP

THE CHALLENGE TO CAPITALISM

- Legitimate economic and moral questions have been raised about the functioning of free markets
- Increasingly, chief executives are powerful advocates of values and ethics in business ... and it no longer seems lip service.

THE TALENT ULTIMATUM
(NETCARE, NETWORK RAIL, CHARITIES AID FOUNDATION)

- When shaping a social agenda, offering expertise can be more effective than writing cheques
- Staff acquire valuable new skills from participation in well-designed social programmes
- The traffic is two-way: third sector collaboration can give access to a vibrant, fertile, creative talent pool.

AT THE CUTTING EDGE
(UK YOUTH PARLIAMENT, CREDIT AGRICOLE, GROUPE DANONE, BUSINESS DISABILITY FORUM)

- Supporting voluntary and community groups can provide insight into the attitudes and behaviours of key cohorts
- Community goodwill is often a prerequisite for commercial success
- Testing new concepts with extreme users can result in more rapid, trouble-free adoption.

REINVENTING PHILANTHROPY
(SOCIAL INVESTMENT BUSINESS, INVESTING FOR GOOD)

- Social investment in an emerging model of financing good causes in response to changing donor and beneficiary needs
- It blends social and economic returns through financial discipline and sector focus, and may eventually offer portfolio management appeal to traditional fund managers
- Tools are now available to assess social impact using robust, standardised measurement criteria.

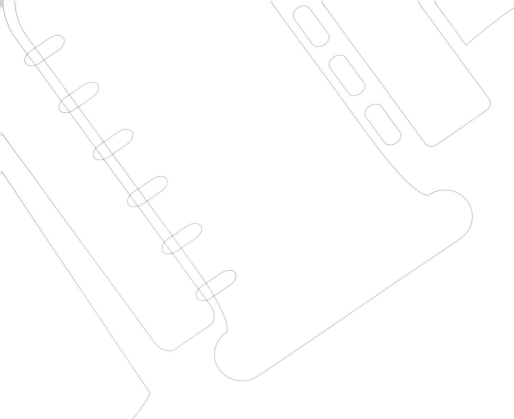

THE CHALLENGE TO CAPITALISM

THE BANNER PROCLAIMING *We are the 99%* had worked itself loose and, sodden from overnight rainfall, lay draped across the steps. Elsewhere, cardboard signs emblazoned with such messages as *Alternatives2Capitalism* and *Your crisis not mine* fluttered in the incessant breeze, generating a restless hum.

For the tourists who had gathered to take pictures with their Polaroids and iPhones, the pinks, purples and greens of weathered tarpaulin created a dramatic contrast with the cathedral's austere Portland stone, like a gaudy kaleidoscope. Harassed commuters pretended not to notice anything amiss, gazing into the middle distance, their pace quickening as they hastened towards the square. Altogether, a typical brisk November morning in the *Occupy London* encampment that had been holding vigil in front of St Paul's for around a month.

During the heady early weeks, the camp retained many of the characteristics of a micro civilisation, with lines of authority, rosters, and an embryonic infrastructure which even included a library, doubling as an information tent. Intrigued to understand the scope and nature of their demands, I approached a clean-shaven twenty-something who introduced himself as 'Tyler' and who seemed to have been entrusted with some responsibility to speak on behalf of the wider movement.

Tyler was thoughtful and articulate throughout our discussion, avoiding histrionics or bluster. And, as the conversation progressed, and we got beyond the litany of formulaic headline demands (stop wars, end oppression, deliver equality), he proved lucid and persuasive in his diagnosis of how capitalism had, on occasion, proved pernicious in its workings and outcomes. In respect of the banking crisis, he challenged the moral and economic logic of effectively socialising losses, after years in which profits had been creamed off by insiders. In respect of the environment, he asked why the planet's assets, forged over millions of years, could be sequestered by favoured corporations for commercial exploitation without recompense or replacement, in acts tantamount to pillage. In respect of consumer power, he argued that voting with one's wallet, in favour of certain enterprises and against others, was a valid expression of free speech, strengthening democracy by giving people a means to express their views outside the five-year parliamentary election cycle. One does not need to accept every tenet of Tyler's manifesto to acknowledge these are legitimate viewpoints that deserve a response.

The Occupy camps are no longer evident around the periphery of St Pauls. They were forcibly evicted in February 2012, shortly after a ruling in favour of the City of London Corporation by the High Court. But Tyler's questions are less easily dismissed. Today, authority figures are less prone to recite glib answers from the establishment crib sheet to the beguiled masses. Instead, a penetrating public spotlight has been focused upon the unintended consequences of unbridled free markets, which not only can function to the detriment of the wider society, but even to the businesses which were apparently riding the wave.

Anthony Jenkins, appointed Chief Executive Officer of *Barclays Bank* in the wake of Bob Diamond's unlamented departure, has placed such store by the need to reincorporate ethics into banking that the *Financial Times* dubbed him 'the Saintly Banker'. "My message to colleagues who won't uphold our values is simple", he wrote in a memo to all 140,000 staff shortly after his appointment, "Barclays is not the place for you."

From pharmaceuticals to consumer electronics, there are examples of organisations now using their values and corporate ideologies to appeal to goals arguably more inspirational than the grubby advancement of the bottom line. Merck calls for "Profit, but profit from work that benefits humanity". For Sony, its endeavours should "Elevate the Japanese culture and national status." Nordstrom's vision is that its contribution should make it "Part of something special." Even cigarette maker Philip Morris (perhaps controversially) places its activity within a broader social context: "The right to personal freedom, to smoke, to buy whatever one wants, is worth defending." Bestselling author Jim Collins has argued that values have a status right alongside purpose as the lasting bedrocks of sustainable success. Using the yin and yang principles from Chinese philosophy (see *Figure 4.1*) to explain that visionary organisations must preserve certain elements at the same time as they change others, he places values firmly, unequivocally in the category that must be constant.

FIGURE 4.1: The role of values in visionary companies

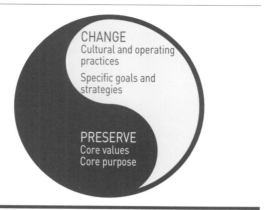

CHANGE
Cultural and operating
practices

Specific goals and
strategies

PRESERVE
Core values
Core purpose

Source: Jim Collins, *Built to Last*

THE TALENT ULTIMATUM

Corporations developing an agenda to benefit the wider community often find that the more effective results come from sharing expertise, rather than writing out cheques for mind-boggling sums with gusto and a dramatic flourish of the Mont Blanc.
We have all seen the grainy images from the 1920s of big business tsars parading oversized cheques in front of the world's media as they scatter their favours upon the downtrodden like the Olympus gods. Bounty transacted in such a manner is seldom used wisely. Perhaps it wends its circuitous way into assorted vanity projects. Or – like the prize money claimed by the early lottery winners – perhaps it wilts under the siege of a thousand grasping outstretched hands.

Netcare is a leading healthcare provider in South Africa, where it operates 55 hospitals (with over 9,000 beds and 300 theatres), and 87 pharmacies. It has been recognised repeatedly for the strength and effectiveness of its social programmes, and it forms part of the Social Responsibility Index of the Johannesburg Stock Exchange. And it has a very clear vision of what it should, and should not, be doing.

Chief Executive Officer, Richard Friedland, is emphatic how necessary it has been, over recent years, to reorientate Netcare's efforts: "Through our separately registered Foundation, we have moved beyond a broad-based social welfare approach that was often reactive to specific requests or major incidents," he says. "Today we're more strategically aligned to the nature of our business. We now concentrate our efforts on healthcare. That is where our expertise lies and where we can make the most significant impact."

Friedland's leadership has led to an increased focus on pro bono emergency medical services, healthcare accessibility initiatives (for example restoring sight to 6000 cataract sufferers), and reconstructive surgical interventions (especially craniofacial abnormalities such as cleft lip and palate). He explains one of the benefits of staying close to Netcare's core competences: "We can facilitate opportunities for our staff to get involved in meaningful projects that improve the well-being of their fellow countrymen. Contributions are made by employees at all levels." This would be more complicated if Netcare's interventions were taking place through abstract and remote channels.

The issue of talent is equally salient for *Network Rail*, the statutory corporation created in 2002 which owns most of the UK's rail infrastructure, including 2,500 stations as well as tracks, signals, tunnels, bridges and level crossings. Suzanne Hardy, who heads up the organisation's community investment strategy, is adamant that social programmes are a proven tool for staff at all levels to acquire valuable new capabilities. "The easy way to release talent involves giving freedom to our own workforce," she says. "We have brilliant people in specialist areas." It's often nigh impossible for local charities dedicated to the preservation of heritage steam railways to afford or access specialisms such as track maintenance or signalling engineers. "When our engineers get involved in local programmes they can learn skills such as mentoring, public speaking and influencing that will be of fantastic value as their careers progress."

Network Rail's determination is that individuals and teams should find ways to work with communities that are not centrally prescribed; this is, Hardy contends, the only way to establish a culture in which staff relish the opportunity to seize responsibility. *Figure 4.2* illustrates Network Rail's continuing journey towards an "involving culture", which demands greater self-reliance amongst all participants, but which – once in situ – is more firmly embedded. For Hardy, a bureaucratic, centralised, top-down community investment programme will stifle rather than stimulate. "The strategy sets guidelines and makes connections. But issues in London are very different from issues in the Scottish Highlands."

FIGURE 4.2: Network Rail's journey towards making an impact that is sustainable

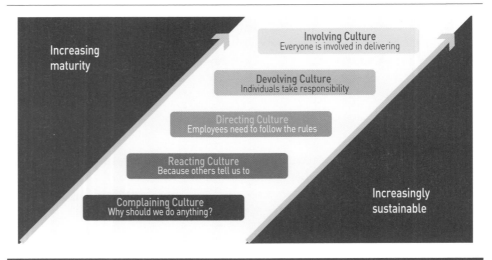

Source: Network Rail

The picture doesn't end with those on Network Rail's payroll. The rail sector comprises a complex architecture of organisations from train operating companies, to platform retailers, to construction companies partnering on major projects such as Crossrail or ThamesLink. Network Rail's statutory role in relation to infrastructure – land, stations, track, property – means it can consider issues and consequences over the long-term. It also places it in a pivotal position to cajole, influence, marshal and arbitrate. "We have finite resources. But we work with literally hundreds of contractors. Either we can all struggle on separately. Or we can work with the entire supply chain to find solutions that are genuinely integrated."

The supply chain discussions have regularly surfaced the pressing issue of the talent gap facing the rail sector. When set against the rising demands of the wider family of stakeholders over the next two decades, a stark and frightening shortfall in the numbers of qualified engineers is projected. "We anticipate a gap of at least 10,000 or 15,000," is Hardy's dramatic conclusion. This challenge can only be effectively addressed when Network Rail works in concert with its supply chain partners. Hence, the final leg to its talent agenda: "In Southwark, we're working with our partners on Future Workforce Skills."

Hardy describes the programme as one part altruism, two parts enlightened self-interest. Representatives from the organisation, and from its partners, have been jointly running sessions in schools and colleges to raise awareness about career opportunities in the rail sector. "We focus on communities that have been affected by our programmes, ones which may not otherwise come across this information," she says. From the basics such as preparing a curriculum vitae and surviving a probationary period, to technical detail such as the sheer range of careers within the sector and the aptitudes that must be displayed and evidenced at interview, the aim is to leave the area enhanced at the end of the project. "A more agile workforce is a positive result," summarises Hardy. "It's good for companies, great for the public that relies upon a functioning railway, and wonderful for the individuals."

Network Rail's example is a world removed from the days when blue chip firms regarded their social problems as a way to sprinkle balm on their collective conscience just prior to the annual bonus round. For Amy Clarke, Head of Advisory at the *Charities Aid Foundation*, such an approach was always muddle-headed. "It's why I'm no fan of terms like philanthropy, that have a slightly Dickensian air," she explains. "When corporates feel pressurised to make a grudging donation, the effects tend to be one-off. You seldom see any ripples across the pond. The potential for mutual benefit lies unfulfilled." If engagement with social causes is one-way, paternalistic and limited, it's scarcely surprising when the wider workforce views such programmes with mounting cynicism. Tertiary and discretionary, the Corporate and Social Responsibility (CSR) programmes of such firms "are vulnerable to the butcher's knife, at the first hint that cutbacks may be imposed," says Clarke.

Lazy social responsibility has been occasionally castigated by commentators such as Dominic Lawson, who in a scathing *Sunday Times* article labelled such practices as nothing more than "theft from shareholders ... a doctrine managed by unelected businessmen and a form of taxation without representation." He raises the suspicion that, in many cases, the goal is less about turning around a social ill, than in securing political kudos or baubles from the palace for executives. The irony of course is that many in the third sector would heartily applaud such sentiments. Clarke spies danger for both the beneficiary and the donor when funds are transacted for a questionable or tainted purpose. "You're not creating a properly beneficial partnership," she asserts. "Sustainable value for both parties is the only effective guarantor of longevity." When Clarke builds a freeway, she expects vehicles to flow in two directions.

There are a number of mechanisms for corporates to realise a return from their participation in social programmes, and – like Friedland and Hardy – Clarke is at pains to emphasise the issue of talent. In her view, firms that are active supporters of social causes are better placed to attract, retain and develop high-calibre performers. And, over time, a more vibrant, creative and fertile talent pool is bound to benefit the organisation strategically. She remarks, "Businesses are in a rut if they compulsively replenish their stock of people with others who look and sound exactly the same. I say, why not disrupt the status quo? Why not look to parts of society that are marginalised or disenfranchised? Firms should have the reach and imagination to hire talent from extraordinary locations."

Clarke argues that recruits from unconventional backgrounds may look at bedevilling problems that perhaps seemed immune to solution in an unconventional manner, and that can be the key to breaking through. Like King Lear raging as the storm clouds gather, organisations can benefit when there's an individual loitering nearby who is prepared to whisper the unpalatable truths that assembled courtiers have preferred to keep under wraps. Someone who can ask tricky questions not because their insight is any better or worse than their colleagues, but simply because their life experience is different.

Developing her theme, Clarke articulates a vision for collaboration between profit-making enterprises and the voluntary and charitable sector that's genuinely two-way, devoid of condescension. She argues with passion for traffic in both directions between corporates and good causes. "Intellectual transfer both ways. Capability development both ways." For her, the promised land involves not merely commercial people sharing with the third sector best practices in, for example, analytical rigour and financial discipline. But also social entrepreneurs showing corporate Britain new ways to innovate, and satisfy needs that lie beyond the scope of this year's profit and loss.

"That's how these ideas get hotwired," she adds. "through a shared interest in meeting the triple bottom line – social, environmental and economic." Her prescription for deep-rooted social change is through individuals and groups engaging in trade, rather than through gifting; mainstream market mechanisms redirected to tackle new challenges. "Community engagement really excites today's high-flyers. When leaders give people the licence to be creative, to ask how to socially engineer a new area so it becomes a viable marketplace," she says. "It's like giving them the keys to the chocolate factory."

AT THE CUTTING EDGE

The *UK Youth Parliament* (UKYP) is a sizzling case study of the hot-wiring philosophy in action. It was established in the late 1990s to provide a platform for young people to campaign on issues where their voice would otherwise be muted. But the team that had nurtured it from conception to launch quickly realised that public sources of finance were welcome but insufficient for the scope of activities they envisaged, including policy campaigns, national outreach and debating events with policymakers and opinion leaders.

One of the pioneers of the UK Youth Parliament, who served as an elected Member of Youth Parliament (MYP), Co-Chairman of the charity's Board of Trustees, and interim Executive Director, was zeitgeist Ashley Sweetland, later awarded an MBE for his role. Recalling the frenetic early days, he comments: "We wanted to be selective and thoughtful in our choice of commercial partners, not roll out the carpet to all-comers. It was important that we built relationships that would stand solid over time. For example, BT partnered with UKYP for eight years; testament to a determination on each side to make it work to the benefit of us both."

As evidence of the collaborative spirit, Sweetland emphasises the regular and open communications between the social enterprise and its financiers. BT's mindset was not to issue its bequest and then retreat from the fray. On the contrary, senior BT managers met with the UKYP leadership on a monthly basis. "These were not one-sided occasions, with BT acting like a sceptical board of directors expecting us to submit endless reports and seek their approval for anything untoward, like some beleaguered ops manager. Not for a moment. The meetings were about understanding what each other was trying to achieve, and identifying where we had shared motivations." Sweetland and his team did of course seek advice from BT's executives, especially on issues where they had so much experience to share. "But they were equally keen to listen to what we said about the attitudes, concerns and priorities of young people."

The rules of engagement for UKYP's donors were clear at outset, documented, and observed both in letter and spirit. At no time did BT, or any other supporter, seek to influence the scope or content of its campaigns, or censure any feedback UKYP might offer. "That would have undermined our worth and legitimacy at a stroke", says Sweetland. As a result, UKYP was able to comment freely on matters such as the operation of BT's apprenticeship scheme, the remit of BT's overall CSR programme, and the ways in which teenagers were using the internet, and the role of social media in how young people communicate with one another and organise their lives. "BT is, of course, in the communications business," says Sweetland. "So there were a legion of areas where UKYP's work was compatible with their objectives. That was the essence of our partnership and BT's support for UKYP's unique platform for young people across the UK."

Within its first decade, UKYP has involved over a million young people in its election process, and influenced national policy in areas including youth involvement on school governing bodies and charitable trustee boards, and even their eligibility to stand in parliamentary elections. These results could not have been achieved if the character of the relationship between UKYP and its business supporters had been one of obsequious supplication, or ingratiating deference. Instead its success stands as testimony to the goodwill, verve and imagination of all around the table.

Within the third sector, fund-raising approaches are evolving so that the commercial boost from participation is clear and unambiguous. Social entrepreneurs recognise that hawking around a crumbling begging bowl with a message of forlorn pleading provides neither an irresistible proposition to potential partners, nor gives access to the type of support that will be of greatest value to the cause over the long term. Before bashing out increasingly desperate entreaties to a cold mailing list of FTSE chief executives, forward-looking not-for-profits now think carefully about the types of spin-off benefits they can deliver, and approach firms selectively to explain their aligned interests. UKYP is a shining example of how supporting voluntary and community groups can provide insights to firms that would otherwise remain buried from view.

Harnessing the enthusiasm and imagination of talented people has led many exemplar institutions to redirect the focus of their social impact activities away from grand, high profile projects. The bank that has arguably received the most accolades for its social programmes in recent years has been France's *Credit Agricole*. While peers such as the ill-fated *RBS Group* were parading their great works in a veritable tome of annual gloss, and former Chief Executive, Fred Goodwin, was being lauded for his high-profile philanthropy, Credit Agricole was stubbornly ploughing an altogether different furrow. Known as *un mécène engagé* (an active patron) it eschewed the glamorous causes, and got stuck in with empowering local managers to choose and support causes that mattered to local communities.

Its vanguard programme, *l'envir d'agir,* involved Credit Agricole putting its resources behind activities as diverse as an antiquities museum, and a professional road cycling team, all chosen through the judgement and knowledge of its local executives. In fact, the bank's commitment to regionalism extends to its very corporate structure. While most listed companies regard small shareholders as at best a nuisance and at worst unhinged, and those that were lumbered with a disproportionate number during bygone privatisations are frenetically engaged in buying back the stock, Credit Agricole positively celebrates its 1.3 million individual shareholders. It lavishes them with consultations and communications. It runs a dedicated 'shareholders corner' on its website. It even employs a Shareholder Relations Team with the delightful mandate of ensuring that shareholders, however insignificant their holding and financial clout, feel treasured, informed and involved; feel, in fact, as proud as should any owner of a valued asset.

Arguably, an even more dramatic example of community engagement was seen a few years ago thousands of miles to the east. *Groupe Danone*, the manufacturer of luxury dairy products such as Activia yoghurts, had been attempting for years to break into the attractive and expanding Indian market, but was struggling to gain acceptance and credibility. While one strand of the organisation wrestled with this challenge, another was based in neighbouring Bangladesh, where it recognised the startling health benefits of the nutrients and vitamins within certain types of yoghurts for malnourished children.

Through a joint venture with Grameen Bank, and using microfinance as the funding mechanism, Danone invested around £100 million in a BREEAM certified factory in Bangladesh, employing local workers on good wages to produce affordable yoghurt targeted at this catchment. As an exercise in enlightenment, self-interest and creative capitalism, it checked a number of boxes. It had an immediate benefit for the target recipients; it met (according to reports) the group's minimal financial threshold; and most significantly in terms of Danone's corporate objectives, it stimulated interest in India, a market that had hitherto been enigmatic and resistant.

In Danone's case, a conventional blunderbuss market entry straight out of the business textbooks, with saturation advertising and hordes of salespeople pummelling distribution channels, would have been the obvious but incorrect solution. A socially purposed vehicle offered a more effective route to foster loyalty and awareness, as a precursor to mainstream product penetration. Smart and imaginative creativity proved superior to template linear thinking in advancing ambitious commercial objectives.

Our odyssey around segments of society that exhibit unconventional needs takes us next into the world of disability. As leader of the *Business Disability Forum*, Susan Scott-Parker has been campaigning for 20 years for businesses to become "disability confident". While acknowledging some progress, she remains bemused by the blinkered attitudes displayed by many boards, whose reflex, when confronted with disability matters, is to parcel them off into a compliance bucket and surround them with the corporate equivalent of the luminous 'do not cross' yellow tape beloved of television homicide detectives.

"Too many times, I hear executives who should know better asking the old tired questions: what are the priorities to help wheelchair users, or those with mental health issues, or those with a visual impairment? I say, let's reframe the debate. Let's ask how they can change their practices to acquire new customers, raise their productivity, minimise their risk. Those are the questions that really matter," says Scott-Parker.

Populations are ageing worldwide, and especially in mature economies. Organisations that make the assumption their every customer is, from head to foot, able-bodied will cut themselves adrift from significant spending power.

With the Business Disability Forum as the catalyst, chief executives from many of the UK's 20 largest firms collated data that was startling in its revelations. They found that a third of Europeans aged between 50 and 65 have a disability of some sort; that UK disabled people have a combined annual spending power exceeding £80 billion; and that – among UK banking customers – 8.3 million have a hearing impairment, 1.7 million have a visual impairment, and 5.8 million are dyslexic. Little wonder that the Business Disability Forum identifies improved retention and product innovation as just two of the benefits accrued by a "disability confident" business (see *Figure 4.3*).

FIGURE 4.3: Five drivers of the Disability Confident business

Source: Business Disability Forum

Effortlessly, Scott-Parker parades a legion of examples where discrimination – carrying a cost in terms of talent, productivity, brand or reputation – has been inadvertent and unthinking, arising simply from the inability of many organisations to join-up their activities, or think through the consequences of their procedures. The facility manager that installed a push button for disabled people to gain elevator access but forgot to inform maintenance about the servicing instructions; the bank that issued cards with the account number displayed using small raised white characters on a cream background; the retailer which conducted nationwide focus groups to assess the impact of self-service checkouts without including a single disabled user amongst the respondents; the recruitment agency that deferred implementation of the Accessible Technology Charter and thereby failed to attract the broadest numbers of suitably qualified applicants for vital placements.

"The best innovation can arise by studying extreme users," Scott-Parker observes. "I remember speaking with the former Director General of *HMRC*. He was determined millions of people should be able to file their taxes online. Noting the reading age of the average tax payer, he reasoned that if his systems worked for users such as those with a visual impairment or dyslexia, they would work better for all. Testing *in extremis* was a powerful beta test on the way to nationwide rollout."

The premise of the Business Disability Forum Charter is commercial benefit rather than diversity, a phrase which Scott-Parker believes most senior leaders position at the margins of their business. Suggesting that firms should only treat people fairly out of a sense of obligation, or even worse because of the force of legislation, is both patronising and misses the central point. With an increasing proportion of the demographic facing access challenges, removing barriers – especially the obstacles of poorly designed property and technology – can lift the revenue top line. "A global

IT firm of my acquaintance was stunned to realise the average age of its purchasers was nearly 50," says Scott-Parker. "Their sales department was filled with twenty-somethings, and this had frankly not occurred to them before."

Charter signatories, from *Barclays* to *Ernst & Young* to *Microsoft*, are all now committed to embedding reasonable adjustments and provide speedy solution for disabled customers, through overcoming internal silos. "Change will not happen if just one department is agitating for it," concludes Scott-Parker. In her experience, firms can realise commercial benefits if they re-gear and are cogniscent of disability amongst their customers and prospects, but this will not happen "without a holistic approach to product development and service delivery."

Human Resources departments that are out of sync with colleagues in Operations or Distribution make negligible impact. A chief executive who understands that ingrained practices are disenfranchising customers can move the needle. He can insist that more imagination is used to crack the challenge of inaccessibility, for example for customers who cannot detect a telephone ring tone, or who struggle with stairs. He may become an advocate for universal design, so that services generically built for customers with no difficulties are refreshed or refashioned, perhaps into "use aware products" (for those with a minor capability loss, including millions of the elderly), to "customisable products" (for those with significant capability loss), to "special purpose products" (for those with complex needs).

The Business Disability Forum's landmark *Realising Potential* blueprint defines this as the "Walk away pound lost every time a customer turns away when confronted by unwelcoming service or inaccessible facilities." This is why its Presidents' Group is populated not with legal and compliance managers, but with chief executives from consumer-obsessed market leaders such as *Sainsbury's* and *BSkyB*.

REINVENTING PHILANTHROPY

Like a modern army taking charge as yesterday's colonels retire, a new generation of philanthropists is arriving on the scene, brimming with ideas about strategy, artillery and manoeuvers. By a magnitude, they're more demanding than their forebears.

The scale of donations, notwithstanding the uncertain economic outlook, remains buoyant. According to analysis by *CapGemini* and *Merrill Lynch*, the global number of high net worth individuals (with over $1 million in investable assets), has risen 8.3 per cent in the past year to around 10.9 million, a third residing in Europe and many more of whom have financial connections with Europe. The combined annual total of charitable giving in the UK from major philanthropists, foundations, corporations and the general population is now approaching £15 billion.

However, the new generation is loath to dispense its resources to good causes on a 'no questions asked' basis, as if posting the quarterly VAT cheque. Many of them have accumulated their wealth through a lifetime in business where they have learnt the value of scrutiny, accountability and scepticism. When considering where and how to make donations, their instinct is to apply the same financial disciplines, ensuring their money is sweated to make the biggest impact. They are squeamish about organisations, however well-intentioned, whose workings are impenetrable and whose results are opaque.

These changes are affecting the supply of capital, but similar movements are detectible on the demand side. Charitable trustees have historically approached financial management tools, including debt, with trepidation. But new appointees – who have often used gearing to build successful businesses in their previous careers – tend to be more open-minded. In a low inflation environment, debt has lost some of its blood-curdling undertones; there are fewer scenarios whereby usurious repayment terms can drive an enterprise to the wall.

And of course the absolute need for funds in the third sector shows no sign of wavering. An ageing population, the consequences of family breakdown, and the pressure of immigration in deprived communities, are all creating challenges. Aware of these trends, the Coalition's policy has been to break the quasi monopoly held for decades by local government to supply social services to the UK's villages, towns and cities. The Social Ventures Act 2012 was legislated in order to encourage greater diversity in provision, with the delivery of vital social, educational and welfare services being opened up, ending exclusive reliance on official bodies.

Social investment emerged at around the turn of the millennium as a new model to bridge the needs of the suppliers of philanthropic funds with those of social enterprise and beneficiaries. It involves intermediating capital into the sector with appropriate financial disciplines to help the emergence of a new class of social entrepreneurs. Crucially, it enables the same donated pound to be put to work multiple times. Intermediaries lend from a pool of donations on either a secured or unsecured basis, and when the loan is cleared it can be rechanneled. The introduction of certain controls and practices from the 'for profit' sector helps focus the recipients on delivering impact, while becoming a more attractive proposition for funding sources, who no longer feel taken for granted. "Social investment is populated with ex-investment banker types," observes Jonathan Jenkins, Chief Executive Officer of the *Social Investment Business Group*, which intermediates capital from central government and other sources into the third sector. "In assessing their investments, they're very focused on testing assumptions and measuring value. It's a useful perspective."

Social investment has fashioned a unique role, with professional intermediaries pursuing a blended social and financial return. *Figure 4.4* depicts the positioning of social investors on the spectrum from grant makers (concerned solely with social return) to mainstream clearers (concerned with maximising financial return). The willingness of social investors to accept a lower – but not *de minimus* – financial return than conventional economics would allow, in return for a different category of impact, has proven compelling for many philanthropists and foundations.

The social investment sector has been expanding by roughly a third every year, and it's currently receiving further impetus from the creation of *Big Society Capital* (a government fund largely built from money in dormant bank accounts), sitting on around £600 million of capital, which it plans to release over time into causes financed by social investment intermediaries. With the arrival of Big Society Capital, the Monitor Institute commented that social investment was on the verge of its third stage of evolution, from "uncoordinated innovation" (2000), to "marketplace building" (2010-2015), and then "maturity", which it defines as the point at which entities can leverage the "fixed costs of their infrastructure" across a "far higher volume of activity."

FIGURE 4.4: The unique role of social investment

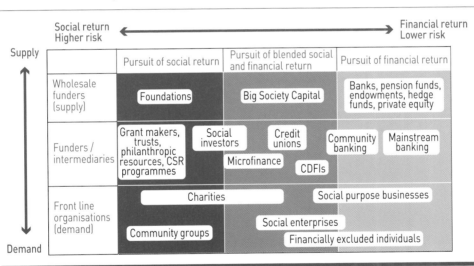

Source: Charities Aid Foundation

Implementing key elements of the Coalition's reforms to public service provision would have been virtually impossible without a functioning social investment market. "Payment By Results has encouraged social entrepreneurs to be more creative and imaginative in thinking about how they can support a particular policy agenda," says Jenkins. "But it's a killer for the working capital of smaller enterprises, and the banks don't want to know. Social investment enables them to gear up to win and deliver contracts before reimbursement is received." *CAF Venturesome*, operating a similar model to intermediate capital, has supported causes such as music education in deprived London boroughs and the provision of work experience to unemployed young people in the West Midlands. "BSC and the rest of the market are determined to make this a sustainable model," says Jenkins. "We can't just burn through the BSC's £600m endowment and then wonder 'where next?'. Everyone is very focused on long-term viability."

As the sector has matured, its leading players have grown clearer in their understanding of its essential pillars and characteristics. Jenkins argues that generalist funds may soon have had their day. "The pressure to measure and to understand the nature of the enterprises we're supporting is leading us towards greater specialisation," he says. "We can develop far tighter metrics when we focus on a niche, such as autism, or penal reform. It can then be meaningful to aggregate the overall impact of the fund over time. You can't do that if you're aggregating numbers about healthcare mortality with numbers about early release reoffending."

Jenkins' vision is that the increased sophistication of the sector will also make it a more attractive proposition for institutional monies. Acknowledging this remains some way off, he sets out a hypothesis that could eventually command credibility with fund managers. "As we establish our track record as a channel for money, I would like to be able to test the correlation of our returns with those of the main market. I have a hunch there will be a limited or no correlation." If this stands up to inspection, Jenkins plans to position social investment as a portfolio management tool. No longer would the providers of capital be asked to accept a dilution in the financial return to reflect social impact. Instead, the message from the sector could be that the returns from social investment, albeit lower than would be priced by a classical risk adjustment calculation, either have no exposure to peaks and troughs, or are in fact counter-cyclical. "As a sector, we're not that far away from being able to run the analysis," Jenkins observes. "If it gives the results I hope, it could be ground-breaking stuff."

As social investment acquired momentum among both supply and demand stakeholders, its pioneers turned their attention to matters of impact assessment. The providers of capital were expressing a gnawing frustration that, once programmes and social ventures received funding, the reporting back was insufficient in its quantum and inadequate in its content. Pressure grew for a coherent analytical framework that could be employed, both by investors and by the social enterprises themselves, to describe how their contributions were delivering impact, the classification of that impact, and of course its magnitude.

Gabi Blumberg is Social Impact Manager with *Investing For Good*, and has worked in the field of impact strategy and planning for many years. She explains the challenge: "Capital providers – whether foundations or philanthropists or corporations – have all become more demanding of social ventures. They are very focused on ensuring their money is making a difference. Yet historically it has been difficult for non-profits to respond to this challenge. There isn't a consistent set of tools they can use. There was no equivalent to the established chart of financial accounts you see in regular businesses. It was a particular problem for the smaller enterprises, who had limited resources, and were directing them exclusively at solving social problems."

Beginning in 2004, Investing For Good launched a debate among key operators in the sector, to correct this omission. Over many years and multiple iterations, they assembled tools that can be used by both the providers and users of social capital. Blumberg summarises the process: "Standardised measures were very important. Investors want to be able to compare like with like. However standardisation is not straightforward; you may have two organisations in the same field that are doing very different things."

An additional complication has been that not all social causes lend themselves to quantification, and it was important not to precipitate a misdirection of capital solely to areas conducive to tight measurement. "Back to work programmes are relatively simple," says Blumberg. "But how do you put a number on time spent looking after elderly people suffering from Alzheimers? That was the puzzle we needed to solve."

After a number of consultations on both the principles of social impact measurement and possible solutions, Blumberg and her colleagues published an Outcomes Matrix. Under thirteen headings, this proposed the most relevant metrics that charities, government, academics and practitioners in each field felt were most practical and insightful. The matrix was commissioned by Big Society Capital, and involved collaboration between Investing for Good, New Philanthropy Capital and The Social Return on Investment Network. The high-level headings are reproduced in *Figure 4.5* (the underlying detail is available on the Investing for Good website). Blumberg is open that the current formulation of the Matrix is work-in-progress, rather than the final word on the subject. As adoption spreads across the sector, the categories will inevitably be refined and revised in light of experience.

FIGURE 4.5: Outcome Map for social investment

Source: Investing For Good

As these types of tools become more accepted and entrenched, there's no reason their application cannot broaden beyond the social investment space. "This is a vital strategic question for us to consider," says Blumberg. There are early mutterings that for profit organisations with a social dimension may, in the coming years, wish to adopt similar concepts. From their different starting points, PLCs and social ventures may find common ground in the conviction that financial returns and impact returns are not mutually exclusive. On many occasions, they can be mutually reinforcing. When Investing For Good released a compendium of their myriad tools in 2012, they quoted from Shakespeare: "If the Prince be too important, tell him there is measure in everything, and so dance out the answer." If commentators are seeking the 21st century's next pivot point, it could be the move into the mainstream of the *blended returns* principle.

THE PHYSICAL LEGACIES of the Occupy movement were swiftly dismantled. I watched as all traces of its presence were eradicated without pity. A battalion of deep cleaning trucks released fumigation equipment as if combatting a zombie apocalypse. Temporary barricades erected from used pallets were razed. Tents were dumped into a convoy of nearby refuse collection lorries. Bailiffs evicted activists with little ceremony; some protested venomously, most felt their moment in the limelight had already exceeded expectations and quietly acquiesced. Within 48 hours, the west front view of St Pauls Cathedral once again resembled that made famous by a million tourist postcards, with its wide open approach, magnificent paired column façade, and famous expanse of steps on which sightseers, lovers, snacking office workers and the occasional pigeon gather.

However, while the material evidence of Tyler and his compatriots has been removed, it does seem that new models of commerce are taking shape which incorporate many of his ideals. The essentials of capitalism will not be supplanted any time soon. Tyler's specific prescriptions – incendiary, passionately argued, often contradictory – are unlikely to become the dominant political narrative in my lifetime.

But subtly, piecemeal, in a thousand ways, the social and economic fabric of society is being refashioned. Unlike his tarpaulin banners fed without mercy into the rotating and compacting grinders of London's finest garbage trucks, Tyler's pleas are not so easily obliterated from the landscape.

5 STRATEGY AND INNOVATION

It is rocket science, after all

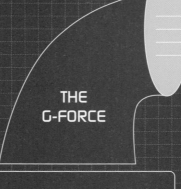

THE
G-FORCE

CUSTOMER VALUE

INNOVATION

SOCIAL IMPACT

THE PROFESSIONS

GOING GLOBAL

STARTING UP

LESSONS IN ROCKET SCIENCE

- Powerful advocacy from a charismatic leader
- Visionaries and practitioners sharing a common purpose
- Purse strings cannot stay tightly tied
- The spur of an evil, conquering competitor.

FROM IDEAS TO MARKET
(XTRAC, KROMEK)

- Faux innovation involves attempts by desperate firms to rebrand ongoing business
- Genuine innovation extends from 'continuous' to 'pivot point' to 'skydiving'
- Continuous innovation combines existing elements in new ways to eke out a better outcome
- Pivot point innovation repositions emerging products to maximise their supply chain impact

WELCOME TO THE FUN HOUSE
(DIANOMI)

- Play has purpose: it teaches flexibility, inventiveness, versatility
- Seven play behaviours can be used to develop and diversify
- Early mover technology players achieved their breakthroughs from experimentation and imagineering

OUTSOURCED INNOVATION
(BRANDJOURNEY)

- Top consumer product giants can be slow to innovate
- Outsourced innovation allows access to a full service platform for bringing new lines to market
- In a digital economy, innovators pursue influence before scale

INNOVATING FOR A HUNDRED YEARS
(H FORMAN & SON)

- In surviving for generations, firms must be able to capitalise on heritage while revitalising for a modern age
- Innovation will never occur unless the culture, set from the leadership, rewards experimentation and initiative
- The mark of innovative firms is this: change is displayed in their every building block, from features to range, to distribution, to branding

CURIOSITY CAME TO rest close to the edge of the Gale crater, and slowly extended an arm. A rock was selected from a small nearby cluster. In careful sequence, it was weighed, measured and photographed. Drilling could now commence.

Decades of DIY enthusiasts would attest that, armed with a trusty Black & Decker, a pair of safety glasses for the nervous novice, and ideally a spirit level, it's generally possible to see the task of creating small holes in everyday materials through to a glorious conclusion within a few minutes. However, *Curiosity* was not being used to erect shelving in a child's bedroom. It was drilling in order to collect materials from inside rocks (surface matter being too degraded) so that onboard precision tools could test for organic carbon compounds. And that was important because *Curiosity* was inspecting samples, as it had been since August 2012, on the surface of the solar system's fourth planet, Mars.

LESSONS IN ROCKET SCIENCE

Operating in alien conditions presented a near-interminable list of challenges for NASA's Mars Exploration Program's team. Perfecting the hammer-wielding motion of the robotic arm required tens of thousands of lines of software to be written and tested at Caltech's Jet Propulsion Laboratory. But that was only the beginning of their odyssey. The conditions on Mars are (naturally) a world away from those of the test environment. Gravitational effects were less powerful. The drill bits were prone to expansion and contraction caused by peak temperatures which often exceeded 180 degrees Fahrenheit. Even powder posed a threat. One of the experts on the program, John Gratzinger, explained the team's terror that dust produced by drilling would "clump and clog the tiny tubes and sieves of our chemical lab." Just one untoward incident could lead to the $3 billion mission being aborted. "We sweated a lot of details."

Of course, the challenges of microbial analysis would be irrelevant had NASA botched the landing. The rover had travelled 350 million miles from Cape Canaveral to the Aeolis Palus, and needed to execute a surface touch down without jeopardising the integrity of its 180 lb payload of scientific instruments. Spectrometers, chromatographs, imagers and radiation assessment detectors are averse to abrupt motion at the best of times. Entry, descent and landing on an alien world are not recommended everyday activities. As the sky crane suspension system prepared the laboratory for final set-down, flight director, Bobak Ferdowski, his 45,000 Twitter followers, the Houston control team, and the thousands watching a live broadcast in New York's Times Square, endured the famous "seven minutes of terror" as they awaited confirmation of a successful outcome. Scarcely can seven minutes have passed at such a plodding, excruciating pace.

It's remarkable that such magnificent results as landing a test laboratory on Mars can be achieved within a fleeting half century of the stuttering, error-strewn early years of the American and Soviet space programmes. In 1967, Moscow had suspended further flying missions after a lone cosmonaut, Vladimir Komarov, had been killed when the new Soyuz spacecraft crashed without warning. In the same year, all three crew members selected for the Apollo 1 mission perished when a cabin fire erupted during a regular launch pad test. Frustrated rescuers spoke in horror of the stench of burned electrical insulation and incinerated plastics, and of dense soot blanketing the once-pristine interior. As investigators worked through the wreckage piece by piece, it became clear that elementary errors had been committed. Pure oxygen was pressurised at 16.7 psi, a frightening level; gasses had somehow leaked from a coolant pipe in close proximity; wire damage had been overlooked in the lower equipment bay, meaning a spark could within moments become the trigger for disaster; and flammable items such as foam pads, left to protect parts of the cabin during the test phase, ignited as if drenched in kerosene. Science journalist Andrew Chaikin pithily concluded the fire was a "disaster waiting to happen."

It's often commented that forging and delivering innovation in business is "not rocket science." But, in fact, many of the levers that enabled NASA to move beyond initial setbacks towards mind-boggling triumphs can be read across to the commercial sphere.

Vitally, there was a clear and audacious vision, articulated not by a mid-ranking flunky but by one of the most charismatic leaders who has ever declaimed from a podium. "I believe this nation should commit itself, before the decade is out, to landing a man on the moon and returning him safely to earth," with these words, spoken with near-evangelical fervour, the young President Kennedy had emboldened a joint session of Congress. "These challenges are embraced", he later added, "not because they are easy, but because they are hard."

Powerful advocacy is, of course, insufficient, otherwise demagogues and dictators would rank foremost in the world's compendiums of innovators. NASA also bought formidable resources to bear to translate the goal into reality. Kennedy not only loosened the purse string; he showered the purse's contents without restraint or forbearance. The space budget rose to 50 cents per person per week for every man, woman and child in the country. Soon, the allocation in a single year exceeded the combined total of the preceding eight. In the months before Neil Armstrong, Buzz Aldrin and Michael Collins climbed in the Apollo 11 Command Module atop 5.6 million pounds of propellant, it's estimated that over 400,000 people were involved in elements of the programme, either at NASA or throughout its network of aerospace contractors.

The third slice of the innovation metaphor is that, with resources secured, there must exist the closest possible alignment between the visionaries and practitioners. Despite his lifelong modesty, Armstrong was essential to the mission for precisely this reason. He was chosen not only because of his aeronautical engineering degree but also his experience as a naval aviator, especially in Korea where he flew 78 missions. If no-one had been around with a practical and pragmatic disposition, determined to match Kennedy's rhetoric with actions and results, then the president's speeches would at best have resulted in an assortment of unworkable novelty sci-fi items languishing in Houston's Aeronautical Heritage Museum. Throughout its history, exceptional performance at NASA has relied upon the coalescing of different disciplines around a single goal – engineers, pilots, geologists, programme managers, procurement experts, physicians – working to a common agenda. This is why, the next time a participant in a product development committee offers the obligatory throwaway remark "it's not rocket science", an apposite response could be "well, sometimes it is."

But there was one further element to Kennedy's challenge. The bogeyman of an evil and all-conquering competitor is a frequent spur to business innovation, as a passionate chief executive uses the spectre of "an enemy who wants to see us dead" to create the imagery of a burning platform which the organisation must overcome. So too with the space programme. And not just any competition, but a race – a "Space

Race" – between the USSR and the United States. As they tussled by proxy to achieve supremacy in space, the super powers hoped this would convert into added impetus for their political sparring on the surface below. For a time, the Soviets made the running. The first artificial satellite, Sputnik 1, was a Soviet launch in 1957. The first living creature in space was a stray dog from the Moscow backstreets named Laikia, who orbited the earth a few months later (but did not long survive the experience). The first human in space was of course Yuri Gagarin, orbiting aboard the Vostok 1 for a momentous 108 minutes. But it was the United States that duly plucked the proudest prize. Its mission to the Sea of Tranquillity arguably heralded not just *Curiosity's* current meanderings around the treacherous ancient Martian streambeds, but also the outcome of the Cold War itself, some 20 years later.

FROM IDEAS TO MARKET

Of course, not every organisation has the vision of Kennedy, the competence of Armstrong, the resources of the American government, or the threat of the USSR. Which is possibly why many organisations are better at paying lip service to innovation than at its delivery. A recent search of annual and quarterly reports filed with the Securities and Exchange Commission revealed that the word innovation was used 33,528 times in a single year. The bulk of these references would not have related to monumental breakthrough changes. Innovation today covers such a spectrum of activities that its impact risks dilution through overuse. Harvard Business School's Clayton Christensen, who wrote in *The Innovator's Dilemma* that successful firms are often reluctant to undermine their star products through substitute solutions, cattily observed that "most companies say they're innovative in the hope they can con investors into thinking there is growth when there isn't."

As shorthand, let us use the term "faux innovation" to describe the type of strategies about which Christensen is so dismissive. In these situations existing products are peddled through existing channels to be used by existing customers for existing purposes; the innovation, such as it is, being justified perhaps through a paint spray, a sexed-up name, or a more enticing pricing strategy. Faux innovation is firmly rooted in the lower left-hand corner of the innovation grid (see *Figure 5.1*).

Moving up the axes, continuous innovation is preferred by organisations that flinch at the risks of moving too far from 'the knitting'. It often involves creating or rearranging connections between elements, rather than introducing new elements. While it may lack the glamour of the top right corner (termed 'skydiving'), it can nevertheless be a credible display of innovation in action. As an approach it also receives sympathetic endorsement from the Austrian economist, Joseph Schumeter, often described as the father of the study of innovation. Schumeter argued that the bulk of innovation entails the creative combination of existing features, products and processes. It rarely involves an idea of brilliant novelty emerging incandescent from thin air like the particles of the Starship commander materialising in the Enterprise's transporter chamber. To Schumeter, that's not a pejorative observation. Innovation by stealth is perfectly acceptable.

Pivot point innovation involves a more dramatic switch. It may mean repositioning an emerging product, which has been struggling to attract custom, to maximise its supply chain impact. It may mean overhauling every element of a business to reorientate it towards different market segments, perhaps taking a commodity brand upmarket, or conversely introducing an exclusive offer to the masses. Such strategies will often require unprecedented changes to designs, features, or functions. But they will be executed for solid commercial reasons that have been subject to scrutiny and evaluation. They're not a leap into the unknown.

For this reason, pivot point innovation is placed slightly adrift of the extreme of the spectrum, where technology is nurtured in the absence of any obvious application; where investment is committed in the hope that when brilliant people invent something brilliant, the market will sort out a need. Cellular biologists push back the boundaries of knowledge remorselessly, but for its own sake; potential applications are only considered once discoveries have been made, if at all. Oceanographers seek knowledge of life forms at unimaginable depths, the last undiscovered inhabitants on earth, with no better answer to the question "why?" than "because it's there." Some state funding is available for such purposes. Among commercial enterprises, the absence of clear application means this is a niche pursuit. "It is the far end of the far end," says Jerel Whittingham (of whom more shortly), "it is the skydiving department".

FIGURE 5.1: From faux to skydiving innovation

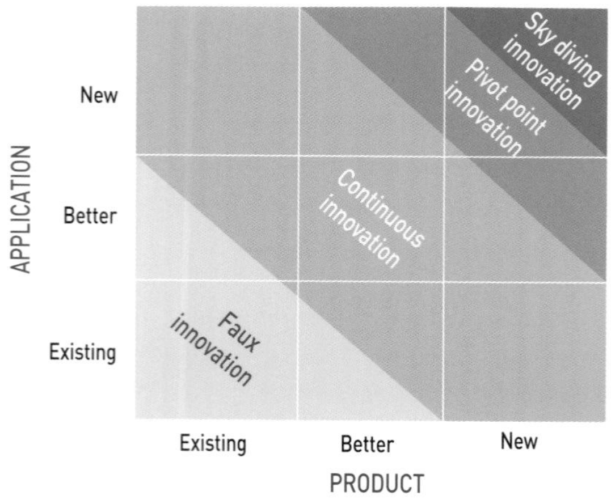

Source: Chase Noble

Some case studies may bring to life these distinctions. Continuous innovation may be the mainstream by comparison with skydiving, but it won't happen without conscious will and deliberate processes. *Xtrac* is a worldwide leader in the design and manufacture of transmission systems for the motorsports market including Formula 1, Le Mans, IndyCar and rallying. Its success is measured in tiny margins; neither faux nor skydiving innovation would be appropriate to its strategic aims. Instead, through simulations and practical tests, it constantly re-engineers every part of the gearbox specification to eke out the last iota of performance. Through examining each stage of production, from turning, to milling, to cutting, to grinding, to polishing, it seeks that one further elusive improvement to aid motorsport drivers across the finishing line a few precious seconds earlier. Challenge and change are integral to its processes; virtually every one of Xtrac's 250-plus headcount is a qualified engineer.

Adrian Moore is the Xtrac Technical Director, with line accountability for both ongoing engineering operations and new developments. For him, Xtrac's strategy embodies the more practical approach to innovation. In Moore's view, a better or different solution is not a random isolated event. Rather, it springs organically from the coalescence of all previous ideas, experiments and attempts. "Firstly we look at the technology roadmap for motorsports, published by the industry body. This covers topics such as hybrid cars, fuel efficiency, lightweight structures, low emissions, embedded communications systems. This gives a useful framework when we brainstorm new projects."

Moore is a powerful advocate of the thesis that effective innovation must leverage established resources and processes, rather than be set up as a class apart. "I've never seen standalone innovation teams as desirable. They can cause resentment, evade accountability, and be so remote that spin-off benefits pass undetected." Instead the practice at Xtrac is to agree collaboratively the innovation ideas that will be supported during the year ahead, and then set up each one as an initiative within the Xtrac Project Delivery framework. "There are clear milestones and projects are ruthlessly culled if we find the technology isn't working or the market isn't there."

This was, for example, the method used by Xtrac to develop its patented seamless gear shift system. A team of engineers identified an early adopter customer located in the United States and worked closely with that firm from prototype stage. "We very rarely innovate if we can't identify a customer; I can't think why we'd do that," muses Moore. For the duration of the project, the customer offered regular feedback – engineers speaking directly to engineers with no sales person acting as part-gatekeeper, part-interloper, and part-maker of unaffordable promises – and also provided both a driver and a vehicle for testing purposes. As the technology approached market readiness, Xtrac's internal processes encouraged a type of corporate osmosis, identifying where this innovation might benefit other product categories. At the firm's monthly Engineering Development meeting, an update from the lead engineer prompted a tsunami of ideas about potential adjacent applications, for example in electric vehicles. This was particularly opportune given the motorsports governing body was on the verge of tightening its regulations on seamless gear shifting, partly undermining the original *causus belli*.

Xtrac operates within a complex network of organisations that have both horizontal and vertical relationships with one another throughout the supply chain. Continuous innovation often cannot be achieved in isolation. It depends upon (and is made more effective by) cooperation between organisations sharing common interests. At Innovate 2011, Professor Eddie Obeng, founder of the Pentacle Business School, drew attention to this widespread feature of innovation. Breakthroughs often require "collaboration between two or more parties" to provide "evolutionary changes in knowledge," Obeng observes. As a result, individual firms are not always the principle actor in the innovation process: "They may not control their own destiny; they may be a bit player in collaboration between users, universities, firms and government."

Xtrac is alert to these dangers, and places great store by careful management of processes throughout the supply chain. For example, it has a decades-long relationship with the specialist steels division of Tata Steel. Operating from a laboratory in the north of England, Tata metallurgists are able to deliver strong, ductile, fatigue-resistant steel, manufactured to remarkable levels of consistency, which can function at high temperatures without performance degradation. "Many of our innovations require us to change the specifications of input materials," explains Moore. "If we need weight savings, or if we're looking at aerospace applications, our supply chain is integral to the efforts. But that presents a knowledge risk. We can outsource the work, but we won't outsource the knowledge. That's a red line." In this instance, Xtrac employs an in-house metallurgist who is effectively part of the extended Tata team, embedded like a CNN reporter accompanying American forces onto the battlefield.

Continuous innovation has worked for Xtrac, but there are many situations where it's insufficient, and organisations must abruptly pivot the product strategy to align it with a new destiny. Earlier in this chapter, we briefly met Jerel Whittingham, and even among technology entrepreneurs, his CV is extraordinary in its breadth and scope. With an academic background in aerospace engineering, supplemented with an MBA from Cranfield, Whittingham has spent 20 years involved as chief executive, non-executive director or mentor with a veritable Aladdin's cave of IP-rich ventures that have upended their sectors. He has worked with technicians, investors and academics to see scientific discoveries applied in the development of new products for the medical diagnostics, security, hardware and space markets. He has helped start-up pioneers with unsurpassed scientific ingenuity but negligible business credibility to secure lavish early stage funding. His track record of board involvement with cutting edge enterprises has included Myconostica (diagnostics), Amphion (life science investment), ROADMap Systems (photonics), and Kromek (colour imaging).

Kromek is a particularly informative case study. The firm was spun out from the Physics Department at Durham University to leverage advances that had been made in the manufacture of various semiconductor materials using CdTe crystals. Whittingham has been involved with the company since its establishment in 2003; over the subsequent ten years, its staffing complement has grown from two to over 100, and its strategy has led it to complete two Stateside acquisitions to secure complementary capabilities as well as a base of operations in the world's largest market. During this period, finalising Kromek's technology has been costly and fraught with unexpected complexities that pushed out timescales. "But," says Whittingham, "that was not the biggest innovation challenge by a long stretch."

In the mid 2000s, Kromek undertook a strategic re-evaluation of the products it had developed and its position in the marketplace. It was now able to manufacture small quantities of high quality semiconductor materials with unique radiation detection properties. It has flirted with licensing. It had negotiated contracts to supply its materials to bodies such as the European Space Agency. However, the board was saddled with this nagging sense that the business model was flawed.

"The product innovation was under control," explains Whittingham. "It worked. But we were not commercialising it in the best way. So we looked at the value chain in the detection market and also in x-ray imaging. We realised that introducing new materials at one point of the chain has a host of knock-on effects elsewhere." Kromek's concern was that it was unreasonable to expect everyone else in the supply chain to adapt processes and behaviours to accommodate its own disruptive technology. Companies such as Microsoft, de Beers, Shell Oil and K-Mart might have the market power to flex their muscles, but early stage entrepreneurs are denied this option. "So we had to move up the chain ourselves, controlling more stages, including software," says Whittingham. "We needed to use our materials' platform to produce sub-assemblies and create end user products. That's why we abruptly changed direction. It's not your conventional type of innovation, but it was the most daring, prescient and ultimately successful move in Kromek's growth story."

To the purist, the business case for pivot point innovation can often appear woefully feeble. The risks can be mountainous; the benefits spurious or ill-defined. But what are often overlooked are the risks of the status quo. The advocates of pivoting are set an impossibly high threshold of evidence they must meet before their recommendations can be endorsed. *Doing nothing* becomes the default strategy, even if the risks of complacency and inertia are more acute and more immediate than the risks of change.

Kromek is poster child for the claim that, occasionally, pivot point innovation can place the firm on a better road to salvation and prosperity. Today, it offers a range of nuclear detection, explosive detection and medical imaging products to the security, healthcare, industrial inspection and defence markets. Great technology is the bedrock: its unique materials solutions owe their existence to Durham University trials conducted over a decade ago in a remote laboratory. At the time, the Durham physicists knew this was no abstract piece of academic introspection; at no point was the research of a skydiving character. They were familiar with the deficiencies of existing detectors and, with due deliberation, sought to rectify them. But, while creating a breakthrough product was a necessary contributor for success, it wasn't sufficient. Commercialisation could only proceed apace when Kromek had figured which stages of the supply chain it needed to control, which it needed to influence, and which it could treat agnostically. Its product reach is now defying expectations, serving such diverse needs as the management of osteoporosis and the detection of radioactive contaminants in foods and liquids. Whittingham concludes, "We're not in the parachute business. Skydiving would have been a step too far."

WELCOME TO THE FUN HOUSE

While the faux/skydiving framework has some practical and evidential underpinnings, it suffers the flaw of many 2x2 or 3x3 matrices. It allows no place for the emotional element of our lives. So let's now turn to the role of play in bringing new ideas and practices to market.

In recent decades, psychiatric consultants such as Stuart L Brown have observed the hitherto unappreciated abundance of play throughout the animal kingdom. They have studied the games of chase enjoyed by juvenile grey wolves in Minnesota, snowball fights initiated by Japanese macaques in Joshinetsu, tussles between leopard mothers and their cubs in Kenya, vivacious leaping by dolphins near Pacific freighters, and dances by Eurasian cranes in Sweden.

As understanding has increased of these forms of play – defined by Brown as "spontaneous behaviour with no clear-cut goal and which does not conform to a stereotypical pattern" – scientists have realised that animals learn flexibility, inventiveness and versatility through play behaviour. These skills help creatures to adapt and endure in often hostile environments. Play is not simply an end in itself; it stimulates the imagination and increases the prospects for survival of both individuals and collectives.

These principles translate directly from the animal kingdom into human society and especially into the strategies of commercial organisations. Brown took time away from his clinical work in the Houston Medical Centre to establish the *National Institute For Play*, with a mission to promote the transformative power of human play (and the dangers inherent in its absence; he noted that homicidal young males in Houston penitentiaries were often deprived of play during their childhood). Building on the work of psychologists such as Jean Piaget and Carl Jung, he has identified seven types of play (see *Figure 5.2*).

FIGURE 5.2: Seven play behaviours

Source: National Institute for Play

Many of these types, especially the more sophisticated levels of play, have an extraordinary relevance for the strategies of any organisation trapped in a Groundhog Day of repetitive, formulaic activity. For example, storytelling play enriches the teller and listener through giving structured narratives to timeless ideas, and allowing oneself through empathy with imagined characters to take part in the unfolding storyline. Transformative play involves germinating new ideas through reshaping our personal experience in a fictional setting. "These play practices ... are essential in organisations capable of producing innovative products and services," says Brown, who has consulted for many years with *Mattel Corporation*, on how to harness the principles of storytelling and transformation, as they develop and diversify their range of toys and games.

One of the UK's most innovative technology companies over the past decade offers firsthand testimony to the veracity of Brown's claims. Cabell de Marcellus, Chief Technology Officer at *Dianomi*, says: "Our greatest breakthroughs came when we were having fun and playing around with ideas. Play is underrated. Without it, I don't think we'd have worked out some really cool stuff."

Dianomi was an early mover in exploiting the potential of online tools and technologies to serve financial brands, financial publishers and the consumers of financial products. It has created a platform, called Exedra, that delivers cost-per-click and cost-per-lead content marketing. Its bluechip client list includes the London Stock Exchange, Yahoo, Bloomberg and over 200 others.

"Experimentation and failure are all part of trying new stuff," explains de Marcellus. "Me and Doc – our Head of IT has an Oxford DPhil, so that's his nickname – we are always knocking around suggestions and thoughts. In fact that's how we stumbled upon our business model itself!"

Today, when such pollination occurs, and innovation starts to bloom, Diamoni staff snap into a different mode of behaviour. "We probe. We challenge. We ask questions. We turn it around," says de Marcellus. In fact, the behaviour can assume an uncanny resemblance to the frenetic experimentation performed on a new plastic toy by a hyperactive toddler, testing (literally) to destruction its durability and functionality.

In my wider consulting experience, I have seen teams using imaginative play to consider how real-life people might react when faced with a new idea. They create hypothetical individuals, such as a successful musician living in Camden, or a land owner in the Caribbean, and ask what a given idea might mean for them. A trick used by one chief executive is to imagine he's standing before an onrushing tidal wave, composed of individuals and families in search of merriment, a wave forcing its way into a fairground just as the gates open. In this dreamlike state, he conceives the *idea* is a coconut shy tucked right inside the entrance. As the scenario unfolds, he wonders what will compel anyone to halt their advance, detach from the wave, and indulge themselves in the idea? Or will they ignore the coconut shy in their surge to reach the waltzers?

Another executive argues that experimentation for its own sake can reveal hidden realms and great treasures. According to this worldview, it can sometimes be dangerous to prototype and test in classic fashion, with anything of questionable value being ruthlessly cleansed, because sometimes customers respond in an unexpected, enthusiastic manner to apparent bugs. Like kindergarten children persevering with their play and wholly oblivious to the plasticine in their hair, the paint on their sweaters, and the adults' scolding words in their ears, so the innovator often needs to blank out naysaying and suspicion. Of course, for reasons of financial expediency, the innovator may sometimes need to don the executioner's mask (when a much-anticipated bloom is exposed as a meagre weed it must be hacked and shredded). But more often the innovator will need mastery of the dark arts of cover stories and double-dealing, in order to nurture a new idea with the necessary nutrients and light up until the moment that it's ready for prime time.

Advertising genius David Ogilvy, founder of the famed Ogilvy and Mather agency where I once worked, said: "Make your thinking as funny as possible." He was not of course suggesting the boardroom should be transformed into the main stage at a Jongleurs comedy club. He was reminding us that, for every one of us, entertainment and humour were formative in our personal development. Banishing them to the outer territories as soon as we cross the threshold into adult work means leaving behind a large part of our very character. It's to the detriment of good thinking; to the detriment of our personal well-being; and ultimately to the detriment of any organisation that needs to adapt to survive or thrive.

OUTSOURCED INNOVATION

The economic resources of consumer product firms can be breathtaking. The top three – *Nestle*, *Proctor and Gamble* and *Unilever* – each enjoy annual sales exceeding $50 billion. If they were nation states, this would place them on par with the annual GDP of mid-ranking countries such as Morocco, Ecuador and Slovakia. The aggregate global sales of the world's top 250 consumer product firms is over $2.5 trillion, coincidentally within a whisker of the entire United Kingdom economy. They are to the modern world what titans such as Oceanus and Gaia were in ancient Greek mythology.

Despite their firepower, these behemoths – much akin to their legendary forebears – can display a cardinal weakness. Their sheer scale can make them ponderously slow. Employing tens of thousands of people across the globe, with a product range running into the hundreds, their very strength can become a source of vulnerability. When opportunities are presented to do things differently, they stutter and stumble. Line extensions and modest product changes are bread and butter; they understand the marketing and operational issues and are able to deliver the necessary changes smoothly. But, when opening up entirely new markets and categories, they wheeze like an off-pace marathon runner. Ideas are trapped in the R&D lab. The racer's junkie hoodlum younger sibling, sentenced to life inside with no prospect of parole.

David Wolfe is a lifelong 'gut entrepreneur' with an irresistible maverick streak. His passion for new challenges has attracted the attentions of many of these consumer product companies. He tells the story: "I noticed how many of them had internal structures and cultures designed to leverage dominant positions. These were not effective when operating on a smaller scale, or for risk-taking or for being nimble. For them, their failure to innovate was becoming a real problem."

For thirty years, blue chip corporations have experimented with different models to break free of their hardwired inertia. From skunkworks to incubation hubs, they have sought the silver bullet that enables projects to proceed unhampered by bureaucracy. Again and again, they have confronted the same obstacle. Career high-flyers have been reluctant to jeopardise their trajectory towards the boardroom by taking responsibility for a new SKU with uncertain prospects, and with a fraction of the marketing budget to which they are accustomed in the core business. NYSE 250 strategy departments are now littered with business plans for breakthrough innovation that never made it off the page.

Wolfe, with his *BrandJourney* colleagues, has introduced to the United States the concept of "outsourced venturing", whereby corporations contract with entrepreneurs to deliver innovation on their behalf. From his Virginia Beach headquarters, he prepares his team for the next assignment with typically idiosyncratic verve – one moment exuding the intensity of a special forces commando on his career-defining mission, the next reclining in his shorts and sneakers with the chilled out air of one who has seen it all before.

"The outsourced venturing principle is straightforward," he explains. "We have a platform to bring new lines to market in under 365 days." The platform begins in conventional fashion, with market diagnostics and customer research to enable a Business Appraisal. When concepts pass this test, and BrandJourney has agreed an acceptable fee-for-service or equity-share arrangement with the sponsoring corporate, the core of the platform is mobilised for Business Formation, Launch, Reinvestment, and ultimately Resale back to the sponsor. BrandJourney has worked in this way with, amongst others, General Mills, the Minneapolis food giant, and Purina, creators of the famed tagline, *Your pet our passion*.

As the platform kicks into action, BrandJourney releases one of its most distinctive capabilities: its cloud-based, modular, plug-and-play technology. "It's brains, heart and lungs combined in one organ," says Wolfe. "This is what delivers revenues fast. New products that might have taken three years to start earning their keep can now be making a positive contribution in a fraction of that time. We call it Digital Gravity." Enabling social networking, e-commerce and customer management to co-mingle in one technological solution, and accessible across devices and browsers, Digital Gravity allows novel propositions to be socialised among early adopters and, only then, rapidly achieve scale.

"The conventional model in corporate America was to pursue scale first and foremost, and almost irrespective of expense," says Wolfe, warming to his theme. "Today's CEO is more accountable. No-one has the stomach any longer for solving problems by throwing money by the bucketload." But the benefit is not primarily financial; securing influence as the first order of business is not only more cost-effective, it also delivers results that are more durable. Market share purchased through deep pockets can plummet the moment the taps are turned off, or someone else arrives on the scene with a bigger howitzer. "Leadership that can only be sustained through blank cheques is not leadership as innovators prize it," concludes Wolfe. *Figure 5.3* visualises how the nature of innovation, especially in the business-to-consumer world, has shifted through the arrival of digital media and the ways that broadcasting thought-provoking content has been democratised.

FIGURE 5.3: Innovation through influence

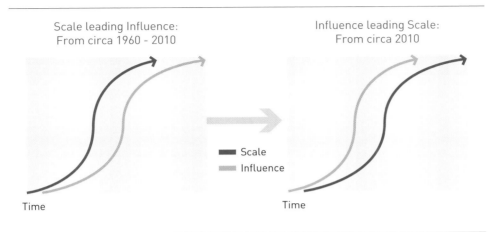

Source: BrandJourney

When communication channels were controlled by a few powerful media tycoons, the barriers to new messages were formidable. Challenger brands would be put back in their place by a barrage of primetime commercials during the Superbowl ($4 million for a 30 second commercial break when the Baltimore Ravens clashed with the San Francisco 49ers). Social media has democratised the power to wield influence. It allows newbies with a compelling message to attract followers. It has elevated content above volume. Today, the innovation land grab is to reach early adopters, secure endorsements from recognised authorities, and be acknowledged as a voice that is shaping the future. Wolfe calls this a "paradigm shift" in the innovator mentality.

INNOVATING FOR ONE HUNDRED YEARS

When annual prizes are awarded to the giants of innovation at conferences and symposiums the summons to take the stage are inevitably issued to engineers, life scientists, information technology professionals or dot com entrepreneurs. Usual suspects such as Apple, Dyson, Google, Boeing or Glaxo SmithKline are routinely trotted out as innovators par excellence. Yet often the most enduring spirit of innovation can be found in more unexpected places.

A family business in the east end of London, employing around 60 people, has been exhibiting this spirit throughout its 100-year history, continually renewing and revitalising itself for a new era, prospering whilst sundry imitators rise, burn out and fall. And it's able to innovate despite operating in one of the oldest industries on the planet: fishery. Isotopic analysis of skeletal remains from the Palaeolithic period reveal that modern humans regularly caught and consumed freshwater fish more than 40,000 years ago. Papyrus documents and hieroglyphs in Luxor crypts show that fresh and dried fish was a staple food for the ancient Egyptian communities gathered around the Nile. *H Forman & Son* purveys its trade conscious of this venerable heritage, but committed to reinventing it for a modern age.

The white heat of 19th century innovation surrounded the firm's genesis when founder Harry Forman arrived in London from Russia. The tradition of curing fish and then applying either cold-smoking or hot-smoking methods had initially been driven by the need to preserve summer fish for consumption around the calendar. Forman's commercial nose and opportunist nature meant he perceived the chance to take the product upmarket. He ceased using fish imported in barrels of brine from the Baltics, and switched to magnificent fresh Scottish salmon. He developed a mild cure that accentuated the taste of the fish rather than the smoke. He doggedly took the results around every outlet within London's culinary establishment. And thus was smoked salmon born as a fine food.

The smoking business may have been handed on from father to son for four generations, yet the instinctive embrace of new ideas and willingness to challenge accepted wisdom has never been compromised. This doesn't mean change for its own sake. When massive smoking factories sprung up in the 1970s, built around salmon farms, and powered by machines that mercilessly drove down the unit costs, a dozen of the East End's traditional smoked salmon purveyors collapsed almost overnight as they over-extended themselves trying to imitate this emergent threat. Formans stuck with traditional artisan techniques, slicing the salmon by knife, while accepting the cost burden as a price of retaining its status delivering products for discerning restaurateurs and hoteliers. But while the Formans' food preparation processes have resisted pressure to change, preferring to capitalise on a distinguished heritage, other aspects of the business have been transformed beyond recognition.

The core smoked salmon offer has been directly affected by Formans' drive to experiment. Where many firms embrace innovation in principle, they keep it remote from the core, parcelling it off in the direction of lacklustre and underperforming products where, frankly, there is no downside. This is not the Formans way. Variants to the core smoked salmon offer aren't permitted under impatient sufferance, they're actively encouraged as a symbol of the firm's confidence and leadership. Head Chef, Lloyd Hardwick, is entreated to indulge his dilettante nature, exploring concepts that might at first blush seem bizarre, but have a better than evens chance of gaining traction. Beetroot-cured salmon, ginger-cured salmon, even gin-and-tonic-cured salmon would never have emerged from the recesses of the right side of his cerebellum had the environment stifled new thinking. "We have a core of 300 customers," explains Harry's great-grandson and current Chief Executive, Lance Forman, "so new ideas don't need a full business case justification. We send them samples, they give us feedback. We can then sit back and watch it go viral."

While his head chef was pushing back boundaries at a product level, Forman himself was preoccupied with applying a similar offbeat, attention-grabbing philosophy to address the most vulnerable aspects of the firm's market position. "Top chefs knew us, but awareness was non-existent among almost any other population," he says. "And I didn't have a million-pound advertising budget, so I needed to do the unexpected. We changed the packaging so it didn't rely on the ubiquitous leaping salmon. Then we created the concept of the discerning gastronome. This sent out a powerful message. It had impact and people remembered us."

Since 1994, every year, Formans has produced and distributed an enormous, quirky, wall-mounted calendar to salmon buyers worldwide. The centrepiece of the calendars has been a distinctive illustration, often with subversive topical references, flaunting how smoked salmon is meant to be enjoyed, in situ, alongside a newly-poured glass of champagne, by the aforesaid gastronome (*Figure 5.4*). "Years before social media, our relationship with our customers became interactive," says Forman. "Chefs were phoning me up throughout the year relaying their suggestions for the next calendar." It was a welcome, if unplanned, consequence of a bravura experiment. "I love that Yiddish expression *Der mentsh trakht un Got lakht* (man plans and God laughs). Never more true than some of our experiences here at Formans."

FIGURE 5.4: H Forman & Son gastronome campaign

In the past decade, almost no small business in the UK has been presented with more opportunities to raise its name awareness than Formans, or leveraged them more precociously. When the British government first mooted a possible bid for the 2012 Summer Olympics, Formans campaigned against a venue that would disrupt hundreds of local firms. When the announcement came on 6 July 2005 that London had been chosen to host, Formans led a high profile media campaign to secure redress for displaced businesses, especially those relying on the indigenous talent pool. And when relocation packages had been negotiated, Formans constructed a salmon-shaped factory on (where else) Fish Island, complete with boutique restaurant and smokehouse gallery, the closest venue to the main Olympic stadium. In officially declaring the new site open for business, London Mayor, Boris Johnson, summarised Formans' status as, quite simply, "a great London business".

Recently, Formans has aimed its pioneering firepower in yet another direction. Through multiple initiatives, it was finding itself closer to the end consumer. It was on the shelves in 75 Waitrose supermarkets, it had invested heavily in its Forman & Field gourmet home delivery and corporate gift hamper business, and it was entertaining diners throughout the age spectrum in its restaurant and lounge bar. "That's when we realised," says Forman, "we faced a newly emerging threat. People resisted paying a premium price for a quality product because there is so much spray-tanned mass produced smoked salmon on the market, smothered with salt and sugar in the factory, injected with brine to increase its weight, then smothered again with lemon in the kitchen. They don't understand any longer what great quality smoked salmon should taste like."

The solution, still being rolled out, has been education. Formans now implements multi-pronged strategies to raise awareness of the gulf that exists between the exceptional and the mundane. Factory tours, public relations, especially in the national tabloids, and television appearances on such programmes as *BBC Celebrity Masterchef* have been driven by the all-consuming ambition to nurture in the public mind the unforgivable folly of transforming a wonderful piece of fish into an alternative so pathetic that copious smoking is the only way the grim evidence can be concealed.

So, on the one hand, innovation can be about NASA-standard breakthrough technology that brings closer the future envisaged by H G Wells or Jules Verne. But the restless ability to look at conventional problems with a new mindset, is, for me, most dramatically evidenced in a thousand family businesses such as Formans, which are testing new ideas, exploring uncharted markets, and diversifying into adjacent disciplines. These firms have nurtured cultures wherein experimentation and initiative are rewarded. Staff don't cower from new ideas lest they fall flat and expose their authors to ridicule. Rather, they fear most the stigma of doing nothing, of flailing in the wake of an industry powering ahead. So they allow change to break free, far beyond the bounds of the little box in the corner labelled 'innovation', to touch every building block of the organisation – from features to range to distribution to branding.

NOT EVERY INNOVATIVE idea will be unprecedented. The opportunity pursued today with vigour and abandon may have occurred to the firm's forebears, or to the predecessor management team. Perhaps the time was not then optimal, or perhaps they shied away from the unknown, like Devon Loch with the 1956 Grand National winning post in view. And surely there can never have been a more pressing time to innovate than in the mid-2010s. Living standards in Europe, including the smallish island off its north-west coast, have stagnated in the face of aggressive competition from dynamic economies in Asia, Africa and Latin America. Presented with such challenges, the temptation to persevere with outmoded notions can have only one gruesome conclusion. Organisations that persist with unwanted solutions to yesterday's concerns don't deserve to survive the coming race. At a minimum, they must continually review the cost and value of their propositions. Beyond that, they may seek a pivot point, relaunching their offer to serve the supply chain in a new capacity. And, on occasion, they may choose skydiving innovation – leaping from the warmth of the plane's interior into a hostile environment where, frankly, humans were never designed to go.

If UK plc is to rise beyond its post-crisis economic travails and lethargy, it will rely upon innovators to inherit the vigour and gusto of President Kennedy. His genius was to make outrageous goals appear within reach. Those who are able to think big, to marshal financial and human resources around a common vision, and to deliver with poise and style, can duly consider themselves inducted as honorary members in the Great Hall of illustrious Rocket Scientists.

6 STRATEGY AND CUSTOMER VALUE
Tashkent or bust

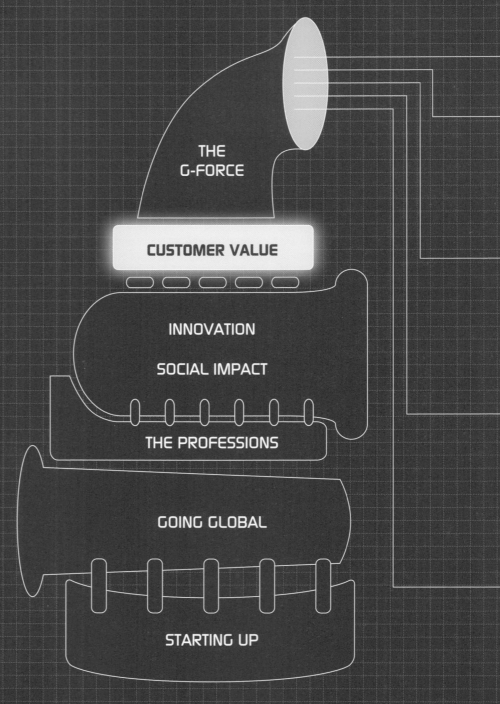

THE
G-FORCE

CUSTOMER VALUE

INNOVATION

SOCIAL IMPACT

THE PROFESSIONS

GOING GLOBAL

STARTING UP

BE COMPELLING!

- Lessons in making oneself the sole, indispensable provider.

SUPERIOR EVC

(ARQIVA)

- Economic Value to the Customer involves more sophisticated financial analysis than upfront price comparison
- How an evidence base trumps theory and hypothesis
- Can a unique selling point be singular? Using a patchwork of unique features to address the requirements of multiple interest groups.

ENGINEERING THE VALUE CHAIN

(TRANSUNION)

- A Value Chain is the sequence of activities that ultimately leads to a customer outcome
- Profit creation can involve the redeployment of investment from one stage of the Value Chain to another
- Firms must understand how their services are being used by customers (up to and including nation states) if they are to maximise value.

UPROOTING THE STATUS QUO

(ROADTOHEALTH)

- Ingrained behaviours make it near impossible to envisage a different solution
- Redesigning a sector from first principles creates unparalleled opportunity to release value
- A web of value can be more durable than the traditional buyer-supplier value exchange; a web involves multiple participants in a symbiotic relationship.

THE BRAND PROMISE

(COFUNDS)

- Brands have distinctive personalities, even in business-to-business
- Successful firms actively manage the rational and emotional levers of their brand, rather than leave the market to reach a judgement
- Value is felt by customers in the heart as well as the wallet.

THE DEPUTY AMBASSADOR yawned loudly, stretching out his chubby hands and revealing underarm sweat which glistened in the faint sunlight. It was a struggle not to stare, especially as the dampness spread. In one armpit the sweat patch was slanted, forking towards the right, taking on a shape that bore a faint resemblance to the Republic of Uzbekistan. I only realised this because a large, frayed map of the country was pinned to the opposite wall. We were, after all, seated in the Uzbek Embassy in London.

"Tell me your story again," he mumbled in the stilted tone of a Bond villain.

"We were here two weeks ago..." I began.

"No. From him. I want to hear it from him," insisted the deputy ambassador, fixing his gaze on Asim, who shuffled uncomfortably. I looked away. To describe the venue as an embassy was technically accurate, I thought, but offered the misleading impression of baroque splendour and pinstriped officialdom. We were certainly not in that type of embassy. A half consumed burger had been left to fester on a paper plate on the window ledge. A musty smell lingered. The only hint of high diplomatic responsibility was that someone had written *Confidential/ government* on a cardboard box which, neglected and unopened, teetered on a shelf. Behind us, in the corner of the room, sat the only other official we had encountered since our arrival. Grey and still, we couldn't be certain she was still alive. On her desk was a mechanical typewriter, a phone, and a glass of water so rank that it might house primordial life forms. She had made no movements that might disturb the serenity of the scene for ten full and ponderous minutes.

I appreciated it was just two years since Uzbekistan had secured its independence. But for all the world, we could have been in the cramped basement office of a 1930s Chicago private investigator rather than the London outpost of a rapidly emerging Central Asian economy.

"It was the last Monday in April," said Asim, emphasising each word. "I met your colleague. I think he was called Mr Nesterov. We told him we hoped to visit your country this summer. He was very friendly and extremely helpful."

The addendum "unlike you" hung unsaid in the air.

Painstakingly, Asim repeated the sequence of events that had bought us to this pass. A fortnight previously, he had spent two hours with Mr Nesterov choreographing how one could spend a week touring from the capital Tashkent around the country. They had studied bus routes and train timetables. They had flicked through the handful of guidebooks now written about the region in search of any hotel with an ample water supply, ideally hot and running. Asim had left with a sketched-out seven day plan, taking in the magnificent ancient city of Samarkand, where we could inspect cultural and architectural legacies from centuries of Silk Road trade between China and the West, as well as the mosques, madrassas and mausoleums of Bukhara, and still allowing time for brief detours into neighbouring Turkmenistan and Kyrgyzstan. He had left exhilarated and abuzz at the adventures that lay ahead.

"This is what Mr Nesterov told us," explained Asim. "He said all I needed to do was sort out flight tickets and he'd issue the visa. That's what we understood. And she was here throughout the discussion." Asim waved half-heartedly at the custodian of the primeval life forms, but knew his efforts to coax her to provide a supporting witness statement was probably futile and certainly desperate. I detected a barely perceptible tilting of her head, but otherwise nothing.

In the early 1990s, during pre-family years, Asim was my regular travelling companion as we explored distant realms in our still-unfulfilled quest to satisfy the membership criteria for the Traveller's Century Club. We had together whitewater rafted down the Zambezi River in the shadows of the thunderous Victoria Falls; feasted in Lahore for five days almost without rest, during the bounteous and life-affirming celebrations that preceded the marriage of the son of a Pakistan Supreme Court judge; and marvelled at the sight of an elephant herd enjoying a waterhole like teenagers in a jacuzzi, against the timeless rolling landscape of the Kruger Game Reserve. He was then, as now, irrepressible, upbeat, exuding excitement about the unknown paths ahead. It has never been in Asim's nature to lament introspectively about unwelcome events, or to remonstrate when others fail to exhibit the charm which, to him, comes naturally. Yet even Asim, I could tell, found retaining his composure when faced with bureaucratic obfuscation required an unprecedented blend of concentration and endeavour.

"I am not Mr Nesterov," the deputy ambassador stonewalled. "You now deal with me. Mr Nesterov has been withdrawn back to Tashkent."

Was the section of the job description about being surly and unhelpful too much for him? I wondered to myself.

"It is very simple what happens next. You must leave your passports with me. You must leave your tickets with me. You must fill out this form I have given you. I will post them back to the Visa Processing Service. I can get that done this afternoon, once you leave." His voice slowed as he exhaled the final three words, unsubtly signalling his impatience with the conversation. He rocked on the swivel chair, and momentarily I feared it would collapse under his weight, impaling him on one of the rusty metal legs.

"But we fly in just ten days," stuttered Asim.

"Pah. It takes at least two months to approve visa applications. You should have them back in July. I can't promise anything faster."

"Is there a fast track service?"

"No fast track service. You must leave the documents and I will send."

Asim and I exchanged rueful glances. We each knew immediately what the other was thinking. Better to spend the next ten days testing to destruction any other options, however outlandish, that we might conjure up, than to surrender ourselves and our passports to the off chance that the Uzbek visa service might, for once, expedite its timelines. Throughout the conversation, I had been balancing on my lap a manila envelope containing our travel documents, health advisory notices, and a recent cliché-ridden *Financial Times* supplement on the country packed with sub-headings that declared "a new era for the country" and "an end to cronyism", which had been the catalyst for the trip. I found my grip on the envelope instinctively tightening, perhaps responding to a subconscious fear the deputy ambassador might make a sudden lunge for my papers. Fortunately, he seemed more interested in stroking away some imaginary annoyance from his earlobe than engaging in physical confrontation. While he fiddled with the ridges of his ear, his chest expanded and a couple of shirt buttons strained as if they were about to burst free. There was clearly no advantage in pursuing visa matters any further.

"Thank you for your time," Asim said as we rose.

"Thank you," I added with unnecessary courtesy.

"My role is to promote trade and tourism. It has been my pleasure to give you this time. That is my purpose," he replied, without rising. Either he found too exhausting this rare interaction with members of the British public, or his mind was already refocusing upon the remaining chunks of his hamburger. I glanced back at the map of the Republic's landlocked terrain, a map that seemed smaller now than when I'd first spotted it. Uzbekistan's cotton farms and folk music and vegetable stews felt more remote and inaccessible. Would we ever set foot on its soil? The life form custodian finally showed signs of mobility, mouthing: "No fast track service," as she followed us to the door and hauled it shut behind us. The latch bolt made a brisk thump.

For the next five days, Asim and I pursued a dozen dead ends in our endeavours to ease our passage into the country. We were left hanging on the long distance telephone line by operatives in virtually every arm of the Uzbek government without once encountering anyone with a modicum of spoken English. We tracked down college friends who had toiled for years for multinational corporations that happened to run activities in Central Asia, in case they were able to facilitate entry. We implored staff at the Foreign and Commonwealth Office to pull non-existent strings. In a pre-internet epoch, we relied on faxes and telex machines to send begging communications to any organisation whose contact details happened to be printed in the *Lonely Planet* guide to the region.

Forty-eight hours prior to flight departure, our mood was near desolate. The abandonment of our mission, once unthinkable, was becoming a real prospect.

"This is nonsense," I said to Asim as we crossed off yet another fruitless lead. "We'll write off the flight costs as a learning experience."

"Don't give up yet," he answered, to keep up his own flagging spirits as much as mine.

"We might be able to bribe our way in," I suggested.

"Don't give up. There's still time," Asim said.

The handset could have been a brick as I summoned the energy to lift it one more time, and redialled the Tashkent Tourist Board. I was now stabbing the numbers on autopilot. During the days since being ushered officiously on our way by the life form custodian, we had learnt that connections can only be established with a remote party in Uzbekistan by enduring a lengthy void, and today the nothingness seemed longer than usual. I was on the verge of terminating the call attempt, when Asim noticed the flick of a green light on the fax machine, indicative of incoming correspondence. As the first couple of inches of thermal paper emerged from the machine, we checked for the sender's address and noticed some flowery Arabic script. This was a novelty.

The rest of the fax was a closely typed message which stated: *I am in receipt. Send me your full names. I send Formal Letter of Invitation. You present at airport. Will allow entry*. It was signed with a single name: *Zafar*.

We read and reread the 23 words in case they contained some hidden meaning we had overlooked. There was no reference to the whims of the Visa Processing Service, which had assumed in our minds the role of ubiquitous pantomime villain. There was no demand to wire money to an anonymous account at a distant credit union. In fact, the communication seemed devoid of bear traps, caveats or disclaimers. It appeared a genuine attempt to help.

"Is there a second page?" I asked, "or is that the end of the message?"

Asim slid his fingers into the guts of the machine to check whether any papers containing further information about the mysterious Zafar had been trapped, but found nothing.

"It looks like Zafar is a man of few words, and he's said his piece. It's up to us to take up the invitation."

I was reading Zafar's communication for a third time. If I correctly interpreted his meaning, all it took was a pro forma invitation from a national, and the thickets of red tape would evaporate into mist. Suddenly, I could almost taste the texture and flavours of the region's renowned patyr bread, freshly emerged from the fires of a traditional clay oven, and coated with garlic, raisins, fried peas and walnuts. The intricate mosaic façade of the Bibi-Khanym Mosque and the imposing minarets that flank it were within reach. There was now the real prospect that our two seats on Saturday's British Airways flight via Istanbul would, after all, not go to waste. Central Asia beckoned, and we had to respond to the call.

Yes, *please*, we scrawled on the nearest sheet of A4, which we shoved a bit too aggressively into the fax despatch tray. *Here are our details. Please reply soonest with the Letter.*

Having almost jammed the machine in our eagerness that no further time be wasted, we both watched transfixed as, line by painful line, our response was scanned, digitised, compressed and transmitted. Ninety minutes later, we were in possession of a document that, for us, combined the grandeur of the Declaration of Independence with the currency of a driving licence. We held in shaking hands a Formal Letter of Invitation for Asim Chaudhri and Laurence Smith, dated May 1994, and signed with a bold flourish by our new best friend, Zafar ("state-approved independent tour guide").

"This calls for a celebration," Asim remarked. "Just nowhere that might attract the attention of the embassy."

BE COMPELLING!

I recalled the Uzbek incident as I started scribbling this chapter on customer value. Asim and I faced the imminent ruin of our carefully wrought plans. Blocked by jobsworths and naysayers, our ambitions were derelict, our flight tickets were worthless slips of card, and our considered verdict on our destination of choice was rapidly becoming unprintable. We were devoid of options, at our wit's end, on the verge of capitulation.

Zafar delivered value on multiple levels. In his role as a state-approved tour guide, he provided a quantified economic return from his service (the per capita travel arrangements topped four figures even before our frustrating showdown with the deputy ambassador). He gave the emotional benefit of a practical, peace-of-mind solution, rather than a restatement of the problem wrapped in a blanket of vague reassurance. He was clear about the next steps. And he ensured he was indispensable to our continuing adventure (the invitation perforce carried his company stamp). Two years beforehand, Uzbekistan languished under the dead hand of Soviet tyranny with commercial enterprise virtually outlawed. When it came to the essentials of customer first, Zafar had been a quick learner. Forge a proposition that imparts demonstrable value, with a compelling appeal both to head and heart, and the rest will follow.

As a postscript, Zafar's endeavours unfortunately didn't always hit the bullseye. His letter proved slightly less of a game-changer than we had hoped at the Tashkent Immigration desk, compelling us to brush off the contingency of handing over a bundle of dollars to avoid summary deportation. Beyond the capital city, his knowledge of his country was woeful, lacking even the piecemeal information we'd picked up during our desk research. And he took the liberty of scheduling our first night's accommodation in an anteroom to Tashkent's finest brothel. Nevertheless, he had provided a vital service when our fortunes were otherwise at a nadir, and we ensured he was generously recompensed before he was covertly dismissed.

SUPERIOR EVC

As if by some unwritten convention, strategists have often invoked the twin variables of purchase price versus quality to determine how their product should be positioned in the marketplace. Using these criteria, the options logically run from 'premium' (high price, high quality), to 'economy' (low price, low quality). Having agreed a positioning, all the ammunition in the firm's arsenal is used in defence of this sacred ground.

Yet, as supply decisions have grown more complex, and procurement analysis has become more precise, sophisticated buyers of products and services have realised that a simplistic trade-off between cost and quality can be fatally unreliable. They are now adept at spotting back-end loaded costs, and rejecting the allure of an apparent bargain basement headline rate. They insist on understanding the full life cost of ownership of the product, through to and including disposal. They scrutinise how the product's features may save them time and money elsewhere. These factors will often be invisible to customers whose cursory study is limited to the sum transacted on day one.

Aware of these issues, Warwick Business School's late Professor Peter Doyle developed the concept of Economic Value to the Customer (EVC). He sought to shatter the traditional two-dimensional scale. His goal was to demonstrate, empirically, that higher prices regularly deliver superior economic value, especially when the financial assessment extends over time and encompasses knock-on effects. In *Marketing Management and Strategy*, he wrote that: "A higher priced product may offer value because it generates more output than a competitor, or because the full-life operating costs are lower." He concluded that, except in commodity markets, short-term price cuts to dislodge a market leader are an unwise course of action. They're often insignificant to the overall value equation. Rightly, customers are wont to remain loyal to existing suppliers, and view with suspicion any offer to switch. The forces of inertia are supreme.

Week after week, Doyle would speak with panache and verve to classes full of MBA students or business executives, listening captivated and with rapt attention to his charismatic evangelising on the nature of customer value. For an incumbent brand, a message about economic value is a surefire way to deter defections. For a challenger brand, he would conclude, a message about economic value is the only compelling route. When an incumbent and challenger meet head-on, the winner will be the firm that has been most lateral and far-reaching in the scope of its value promise. Post-purchase costs such as servicing, maintenance and energy consumption are self-evidently part of the analysis, but the story need not end there. "Besides lowering a customer's costs, a product may also enhance its revenues," argued Doyle. "That's why EVC is a powerful tool but it demands a sophisticated sales force that's adept at analysing value chains." If the sales person can't get to grips with the customer's intended use of the product, their canvass will suffer self-imposed limitations. *Figure 6.1* shows the scope to raise EVC in a hypothetical sales situation from a mere £30,000 to £70,000 through the appreciation of such added value potential. Such insights can, for example, enable luxury fountain pens to be priced not in relation to their cost of manufacture, or to other writing instruments, but in relation to the multi-million pound contract the pen will be used to sign.

FIGURE 6.1: Economic value to the customer

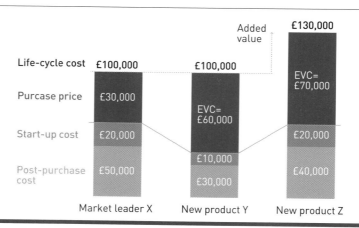

Source: Peter Doyle, *Marketing Management and Strategy*

Paul Warminger was a Professor Doyle protégé. In the 1980s, upon graduation from the Warwick MBA programme, he was awarded the prestigious annual marketing prize. Decades later, he's still applying the principles of value formulation and communication that he learnt studying at the feet of the maestro, working with *Arqiva* – the communications infrastructure and media services company, which has provided pioneering transmission capabilities to the television and mobile phone sector. Having recently managed a bid for a 15-year contract for a wider programme destined to deliver around £7 billion in net benefits to multiple stakeholders, Warminger today knows as much about this subject as anyone else in the country.

With the bid submitted, there was little to do but await the final pronouncement. Arqiva's vast 'war room', which at the peak of activity had been home to almost 100 frenetic engineers, analysts, pitch experts and advisers, was now eerily deserted. Secure areas whose walls have been plastered with storyboards stood vacant. Demonstration suites were empty. For Warminger, it was akin to being the controller left alone in the silent void of the military aircraft hangar while the Spitfire fleet is out on manoeuvers.

Arqiva was the lead contractor supported by technology firms Sensus and EDMI which had been pitching to run the Communication Services at the heart of the rollout of smart metering to every home in Great Britain. The challenge, set by the *Department of Energy and Climate Change* to the energy industry, was to implement technologies that aid the country's transition to a low carbon economy. The assumption behind the programme is that near real-time information on energy consumption would help householders to control their energy use, and energy firms to more effectively manage their energy networks and to innovate new consumer services. The scheme's stated objective is that by 2020 more than 50 million smart meters will have been installed in over 30 million properties.

"With a bid of this size and complexity, we could not compete as the lowest cost option," says Warminger. "A price only driven procurement would have squeezed our margins and made it harder to recoup our bid costs. On the other hand, we knew cost was a key criterion in the selection process, and we would need to justify the economic value of every pound. That meant it was essential to understand the full range of value drivers within the programme. It took us almost four years, from intensive periods of Government and industry consultation, to the first pre-qualification questionnaire, to build a proven technical and commercial proposition in which every one of these factors was properly reflected."

In order to demonstrate the value of the consortium's solution, Warminger knew that theory and hypotheses would be insufficient. He and his team built prototypes, ran GB-based field trials, stress-tested security issues, and assessed the impact on consumer experience of technologies, service levels and installation processes. "That's what's meant by an evidence-based procurement," says Warminger. "Evaluators' eyes glaze over at fine words without robust back up. We undertook in-depth, empirical research among every category of users, geography and building types. We were supported by suppliers and the energy providers to install our equipment and service architecture on a test basis. We modelled the results and subjected them to independent verification. It was very thorough."

The Arqiva solution addresses, head-on and on multiple levels, how the publicly stated vision of multi-billion in net benefits could be supported. *Figure 6.2* presents a summary of the value proposition that was included in the submission. Firstly, Arqiva placed centre-stage the promise of "lowest Total Cost of Ownership over 15 years", which considered industry's costs to install and maintain rather than focusing on the up-front price. It sought to lock-in this baseline aspiration as the minimum acceptable outcome. Their technology was based on the creation of a dedicated platform with no competing uses, and provided near universal coverage without reliance on potential patchy reception of competing technologies. Secondly, crucially, Arqiva argued that additional value, far in excess of the envisaged £7 billion, could also be secured. "The technology has multiple future "Machine-to-Machine" applications, such as water metering, and smarter grids; we are laying the foundations of the smart city," explains Warminger.

FIGURE 6.2: Arqiva value proposition

Proposition: A dedicated, universal, secure, resilient, end-to-end Smart Metering solution – designed to endure – that is uniquely suited to the requirements for a critical national infrastructure, delivering the lowest long-term total cost of ownership and enabling Smart Metering, Smart Grid and Smart Water. Means lowest Total Cost of Ownership over a 15-year horizon.

Unique benefits:

- Proven long-range radio solution providing near 100 per cent meter location national coverage, with dedicated spectrum for life of network asset

- Dedicated network with pre-existing smart metering functionality for extra performance, resilience and security

- Direct to meter option for utility independence

- Ability to support high SLA demands for connectivity, short message latency and availability

- End-to-end delivery assurance from a leading communications network services provider offers single point of accountability

- A platform for consumer services

Additional benefits:

- More competitive price than you might think (right first time install process)

- Long-term cost certainty

- A sustainable supply chain with established reputation and experience; in this for the long-term

- Long-term solution minimises consumer disruption

- Proven additional uses for Smart Water and Smart Grid

- Enables "beyond the meter" in-home networks and technology.

Source: Arqiva, reproduced with permission

There was a further complication for Arqiva in demonstrating the economic value for customers. The rollout of smart metering involved multiple interest groups. There was no one single all-powerful customer whose needs were paramount and took precedence over all other onlookers.

The government was taking the lead role in the procurement; the industry was bearing the cost of the programme; and consumers were the principle beneficiaries. Each of these interest groups was focused on different aspects of the solution: security, longevity, coverage, speed, price, performance, versatility. In one exercise, Arqiva identified 23 separate groups of stakeholders, from the 'Big Six' energy suppliers, to the regulator, small retailers, consumer groups, and a veritable Guatemalan rainforest of acronyms (DNOs, MOPs, MAPs, MAMs, EUA, ICoSS, GSMA and the rest). The unique selling point could not be singular.

Instead, a patchwork of unique features would need to address the requirements of multiple parties. During the final review stage, Warminger painstakingly ensured the concerns of each stakeholder had been addressed to his satisfaction. These included a belief in one quarter that speed to market could not be compromised; demonstrate that Arqiva would achieve 80 per cent coverage at meter point locations at network Go-Live and almost ubiquitous coverage within 18 months thereafter; a concern about data security and confidentiality; show that Arqiva's proposed communications network isn't simply another application of the existing fixed and mobile networks, but actually an addition to Britain's critical national infrastructure (CNI). "The core value message was consistent: our network is dedicated, universal, secure, resilient, end-to-end," says Warminger. "But we did need to finesse the emphasis. And raise our sights. There's increasing acceptance that, in the UK's expedition toward an intelligent information infrastructure, £7 billion in benefits is merely the down payment."

In September 2013, Arqiva signed a circa 1,500 page contract to implement its technology throughout the north of England and Scotland. The adventure was underway. Smart Metering was arriving in Great Britain.

ENGINEERING THE VALUE CHAIN

While Warminger was modelling early concepts of Economic Value to the Customer, on the other side of the Atlantic, strategy boutiques such as the *Boston Consulting Group (BCG)* were honing their understanding of Value Chain management. The premise of the Value Chain is that customer outcomes often result from a complex sequence of activities. Every stage of this sequence absorbs a proportion of cost, and ties up a proportion of capital. Ideally, it should always generate incremental Value in excess of this expense, although profit realisation is not necessarily shared fairly and equitably throughout the chain.

For strategists, mapping the entire Value Chain in a sector is akin to the efforts of scientists to map the human genome sequence. In the latter group, geneticists such as Professor Ian Tomlinson at the Wellcome Trust Centre analyse DNA repair polymorphisms to identify systematic weaknesses that can be remedied. In the former group, firms use a host of analytics tools to model competitive intensity and profit potential throughout the Value Chain, from the supply of raw components to the assembly of the finished product. They can dial up or dial down their investment in different stages of the chain, redeploying capital to its greatest effect. If Archimedes of Syracuse had been born in 20th century Boston, rather than over 2,000 years beforehand in Sicily, it might have been mapping the Value Chain rather than displacing water that led to the iconic exclamation of "Eureka!"

During those heady days, David Neenan was learning his trade as an upcoming BCG consultant. He saw the transformative power of Value Chain analysis in making strategic decisions about the development of retail banking. It revealed options for extending or withdrawing the banking footprint. Decisions on product development, line extensions, acquisitions and automation were all informed by Value Chain modelling.

Neenan is now the International President of *TransUnion*, one of the world's largest credit reporting agencies with over 45,000 corporate clients. He's responsible for operations in 33 countries outside the United States, including fast-emerging dynamos such as Brazil and India, where data is patchy, prospects are dizzying, and regulators are wrestling to impose arrangements which will deter western-style bubbles. In this role, he still sets aside time to cogitate about the Value Chain in which he participates, and figure out how to influence its continued evolution.

"We're now active in at least five stages of the Value Chain," explains Neenan. "Pre-screening means banks mail offers to customers they already know are attractive, slashing the underwriting and marketing expense. Acquisition checks validate the risk and optimise the response, rooting out attempted frauds and highlighting where further investigation is merited. Portfolio management tracks this year's vintage against last year's, so that strategies can be adjusted. Collection gives early warning of where risks may materialise so lines can be reduced or other pre-emptive actions undertaken. And dynamic marketing completes the circle, responding to known triggers with targeted offers. Our longevity in this market is founded on the fact we have a proposition for each stage of the loan cycle. If we were a bit part player, we would have been squeezed out." *Figure 6.3* shows the relationship between the loan life cycle and the TransUnion proposition.

FIGURE 6.3: Credit bureau Value Chain proposition

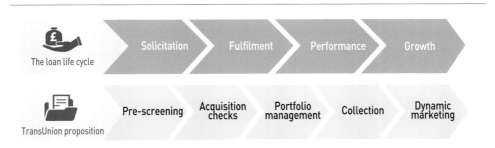

Source: TransUnion, Chase Noble analysis

Value Chain management means the role of credit bureaus such as TransUnion is now light years away from the era of card files in steel cabinets (legend has it the firm's entire knowledge base was once contained in 400 such units). TransUnion now takes raw data from up to 80 sources. It triangulates, matches, and cross-tabulates to fine-tune its scorings prior to release.

Powerful technology runs like a golden thread throughout each of Neenan's five stages. Processing muscle has dramatically slashed the costs of analytics. The capacity of microprocessors has increased speed; computations that took hours are now measured in nanoseconds. Road-tested algorithms mean results are more reliable. And, most recently, with the advent of Big Data, technology systems are able to mimic the human competence in fuzzy logic – using a type of sophisticated intuition to spot causal connections that were not immediately evident. Controlling each of these stages of "the data chain" enables firms such as TransUnion to offer a powerful series of messages to their customers. They now have choices. At one price point, they can offer a basic reactive data service, using predefined criteria, at the level of the individual applicant. At a different price point, they can work with clients at a more holistic level, interpreting the overall data trends, and testing new criteria and variables.

For Neenan, the decision to compete at five stages of the credit Value Chain has taken TransUnion's offer to a new level. But the journey isn't yet complete. Stages such as pre-screening, collection and dynamic marketing are essential ingredients, not the finished meal. Credit bureaus will remain shackled by their legacy of supplying semi-commoditised information unless their relationship with their clients becomes even more intimate. The next challenge, for Neenan, is to understand – not at a superficial level, but with meticulous rigour and tenacity – the strategic issues within clients that rely upon accurate, real time, insightful data analytics. That's the key to refocusing their clients' attention away from cost in favour of the value multiplier. The few dollars a mortgage provider might pay for a credit report becomes almost insignificant. The data is being used for decisions where tens, perhaps hundreds, of thousands of dollars might be at stake. That's the difference between advancing funds to a reliable borrower compared with one prone to default.

The goal is the repositioning of credit bureaus as strategic partners rather than information sources. Neenan foresees a Tipping Point. "Look at how similar approaches have revolutionised other sectors. IBM don't just supply boxes anymore; they saw how clients were using computers and so acquired PwC so they could offer solutions. When HP understood how photocopiers were being used, they moved into document management." For this reason, Neenan is currently overhauling his sales machine, recruiting individuals with the imagination, inclination and experiences to engage in more strategic discussions with clients. "An early result of this approach is that we can now operate decision tools for our clients. We're the ones giving *go/no go* answers based on agreed criteria." It's also what drove TransUnion to intensify its penetration of adjacent sectors where data analytics can make a tangible difference to outcomes: auto insurance, property management and healthcare.

A few years ago, the buzz phrase in strategy circles was the concept of the Big Hairy Audacious Goal (BHAG). And they don't come much more audacious than this. Having spread their investment across multiple stages of the Value Chain for loans and mortgages, TransUnion recognised the chain was but one of many. Far beyond these narrow realms, modern society is overflowing with data analytics Value Chains. Neenan fizzes with enthusiasm for this challenge.

And audacity doesn't come much bigger and hairier than using analytics to assist the economic development of the nation state. The turmoil in global financial markets since 2007 has proven beyond riposte that the international community has a legitimate interest in effective credit scoring. Its value is not limited to the commercial interests of loan makers and recipients. Credit scoring props up worldwide financial stability. It's also a cog, perhaps the most indispensable cog, enabling under-developed economies to switch into overdrive. Without credit scoring, banks cannot adjust interest rates to reflect individual risk, so entrepreneurial risk-taking is deterred. Without credit scoring, banks are forced to rely on antiquated methods such as time on file, and suffer the inevitable charge-offs from perverse decisions. Without credit scoring, the middle class struggles to create a viable tier between the elite possessing, and often abusing, extreme wealth, and the mass of the population on barely subsistence wages.

So TransUnion's international growth trajectory is also based on understanding the value of its data to the political and economic vision; to the narrative of high potential nation states. "The practice of lazy lending holds back tiger economies, but since 2007 local regulators have been forcing them to raise their standards. They don't want another blow up," says Neenan with decisive emphasis. "I'm struck by how quickly the leaders in regions such as South America and the Indian subcontinent are embracing the ways data analytics can deliver economic advancement. Now that's what I call a Tipping Point!"

UPROOTING THE STATUS QUO

We are all creatures of habit. Complex sets of behaviours and assumptions become so ingrained in the ways we live that we find it near impossible to envisage a different way. Inherited norms are unchallengeable because they are embedded in our worldview. The status quo acquires a tone of reassurance. Step changes, our instincts cry out, are unnecessary and fraught with peril. Trickster illusionists, such as Derren Brown, play endlessly upon our grotesque failures of imagination. Brown uses a combination of suggestion, psychology and misdirection to deliver outcomes that seem beyond the realm of our practical experience. In our daily lives, individuals are unable to select the random word we have just secretly written down; they cannot reproduce exactly a skyline they only observed for 15 seconds. When we cannot fathom Brown's methods from any point of reference at our disposal, we abandon the attempt. We succumb and weakly confess that magic is the only remaining explanation.

Many sectors of the modern British economy survive in their current form for no better reason than that, decades ago, they came into being a certain way. Technology, social norms, and even empirical evidence may have undermined the raison d'etre; nevertheless, it can be fiendishly difficult to unravel long accepted legacies and the many entrenched and vocal interest groups that benefit from inherited practices.

Redesigning a sector from first principles creates unparalleled opportunities to release value, and health screening is a case in point. Most readers will have undergone a screening at some point in their lives, perhaps as part of a pre-employment check, perhaps when applying for life insurance. For decades, the process was fixed in aspic. A nurse would drive to your home, usually arriving at the least convenient moment (amidst blazing rows about remote control ownership), unload her carrier bag of stethoscopes, test tubes, and needles across the kitchen table, carefully take three blood pressure readings, collect assorted samples, and then gaily depart for the next appointment. During the decades, revolutionary changes were elsewhere underway. The internet was born and grew ubiquitous. Retail healthcare services sprang up on every high street. Medical science unleashed the predictive potential of diagnostics. Yet still the nurse would travel, at great expense, to your home to perform the same unchanging rituals.

Alistair Wickens, along with two other entrepreneurs, observed the market with growing frustration. They were convinced a better way must exist. They embarked upon a series of discussions with the purchasers of health screening (starting with insurers) and pharmacy groups – the latter owning a national network of clinical facilities on almost every High Street staffed by trained professionals. Wickens and his team started to map out the contours of a better solution. A new model, he realised, could not be created by simply tinkering at the edges of the home visit, hospital or private health clinic method. Every assumption about the conduct of screenings must be discarded. The sector needed to be redesigned as if from scratch. The canard "I wouldn't have started from here" was Wickens' opportunity. Launching the business, *roadtohealth*, the team defiantly did not "start from here" (although they faced an uphill challenge in persuading dozens of market participants that neither did they). Starting from a very different place, reconstituting an established sector from first principles, created enormous opportunities to release and share new sources of value.

Ten years later, with expanding operations in the UK, Australia, the United States, mainland Europe and South East Asia, roadtohealth has taken things one stage further by removing the need for physical screening with intelligent, online health assessments which empower millions of users to carry out simple and clinically-validated online health assessment using mobile devices – linked to thousands of clinical professionals where clinical interventions are required. Of greater economic value to insurers, and of greater medical value to the public.

"We devised a method, called the Q Score, which places individuals in a queue of 100 people of the same sex and age, with the person closest to 100 having the lowest risk of developing specific disease states over the next 10 years" explains Wickens. "Once you understand your health risk, we can offer highly personalised health intervention programmes to improve your Q score and reduce your risk. This is of huge benefit to any organisation with a vested interest in improving the health of a population."

The film's web presence was vital to its restructuring of value distribution within the sector. Value no longer entails a simple binary transaction between the supplier of a service and the purchaser. In its place, roadtohealth has created a network of value exchange between multiple participants existing in almost a symbiotic relationship with one another.

As a result, roadtohealth delivers economic value to insurers and corporates because using clinically-validated online services has slashed the unit cost of delivery to virtually nil, compared with more costly and traditional ways of assessing health risk and gathering healthcare data. The programmes deliver value to each end-user, as they gain a detailed insight into their future health risk with timely, relevant and achievable tips, health improvement trackers and challenges to keep them moving towards a healthier lifestyle. In fact, one interesting turn of events is that insurers are using roadtohealth to engage with their customers on a weekly basis, whereas previously this was an annual event which coincided with the renewal of a policy. End users engage with the programmes for their own personal gain and, in some cases, insurers reward individuals with financial incentives through premium discount if there are improvements in health risk over a period of time. This is a perfect win:win scenario, brought about by re-engineering the way the sector approaches the issues of gathering medical underwriting data and maintaining regular and meaningful engagement with their customers. In the centre of this architecture is roadtohealth – facilitating, aggregating, providing the infrastructure, and gradually assembling an incredibly potent database of health, lifestyle statistics and demographic data.

In summary, roadtohealth is one of the United Kingdom's purest examples of how online technologies can reinvent value exchange. For many established firms, the world wide web simply means uploading content, or phasing out brochures in favour of a digital homepage, or replacing paper correspondence with a blizzard of emails. But in the case of roadtohealth, the internet (and more recently, app-based technology via mobile devices) has provided a channel to deliver a suite of services that were once logistically and commercially untenable. More exciting still, for Wickens, is that the journey has barely begun. "I see roadtohealth being transformed into an organisation which is able to provide really detailed insights into the health and lifestyle data of individuals or groups. With the launch of new direct-to-consumer versions of our programme, we're building a phenomenal data-rich asset. In that respect, we're becoming an unassailable resource." Data will, Wickens envisages, become the fundamental value-driver for roadtohealth – a fact reinforced by the number of approaches by potential purchasers since the company launched its data strategy in 2012.

Having started the journey by recreating the health screening value model, roadtohealth has built a successful international business, aggregating a number of service providers, and providing them with a common platform from which they all derive value. They've also found a method to engage with the customer repeatedly over time. In doing so, they have created an ever-increasing data asset which, alongside the complex architecture of relationships in place, will be a powerful deterrent to competitive entry over the coming years.

THE BRAND PROMISE

In the 1990s, working as an independent financial adviser (IFA) not only required the category skills of counselling, analysis and communication, but also a peerless passion for administration. For one day each week, the adviser withdrew like a hermit crab from the cut and thrust of financial planning, surrounded himself or herself with teetering piles of paperwork, and embarked upon a marathon of form-filling, record-keeping, reconciliation-posting, certificate-processing, signature-chasing, and insurer-liaising. IFAs are not a species generally worthy of grand outpourings of sympathy, but the thankless bureaucracy that was – until recently – disgorged from the simplest transaction was relentless and mind-numbing.

Into this world of red tape sprang *Cofunds*, one of the first, and quickly the largest, of the two dozen platform providers that now service the IFA sector. The platform premise is straightforward: it provides a web-based solution for advisers to aggregate the investments of their customers in one place. Benefits include more effective management of a portfolio since consolidated valuations can be generated in real time, switching between and within funds can be processed rapidly, and tools can be deployed to benchmark risk and performance against key indices. Around one-third of

IFAs in the country now take advantage of the Cofunds platform, on behalf of nearly one million end investors. Stephen Wynne-Jones, Head of Marketing Operations at Cofunds, describes the concept: "We offer an aggregation service. Everything is pulled into one place. Underpinned with robust technology, this enables transactions to happen more quickly and more cheaply. It's an economic argument, and it's also about peace of mind." This deployment of both rational and emotional factors – this simultaneous appeal to both the heart and wallet – has been a constant theme throughout Cofund's history.

Cofunds erupted from the starting gate in a flurry of excitement, and quickly won fans and attention. As in any young but fast-developing marketplace, potential competitors were struck by this early success, and set up in rivalry. The new entrants came in all shapes and sizes – some promoted their independence, some their specialisation, some their powerhouse technology. IFAs began to experiment. But while the market was in its immature phase, certain attributes worked strongly in Cofunds' favour. It was widely known as "plucky little Cofunds", taking up the battle on behalf of small advisory firms against a herd of belligerent faceless corporate behemoths. It commanded affection and loyalty, enabling it to ride out any occasional setback. Advisers were "on its side", willing Cofunds forward, inspired by the vision of a near-paperless future. It was inconceivable they would defect on a whim, or tender out platform services, so the alternatives fought for supremacy like proverbial ferrets. Cofunds, to them, was a business partner. These emotional bonds helped the firm withstand many typical early stage growing pains.

Roll forward a decade and the tag "plucky little Cofunds" has passed its sell-by date. With £50 billion of assets held on the platform, the moniker *little* was no longer applicable. Neither did the *plucky outsider* concept have quite the same resonance; if anything, it was the dominant market player fending off insurgents.

During 2011, and again in 2013, Cofunds embarked upon a research programme to discover precisely how perceptions of its brand value had morphed over ten years. Much of this involved mystery shopping; one hour depth interviews between advisers and independent consultants, with Cofunds' identity withheld in order to avoid bias in the responses.

Wynne Jones described the purpose. "There is a risk, inherent in being market leader, that firms become complacent. They're afraid to shake things up, lest they upset what's working. This exercise was squarely designed to stop Cofunds falling into that trap."

The research explored every facet of customer value, from the role of the sector in serving unmet needs, to the market's perception of Cofunds in relation to its peer group (market position, proposition, business model), and concluding with strategic choices and priorities for further added value. At the heart of the framework stands 'proposition', and at the heart of the proposition stands 'brand personality'. All 15 components of the framework are reproduced in *Figure 6.4*.

FIGURE 6.4: Cofunds' customer value framework

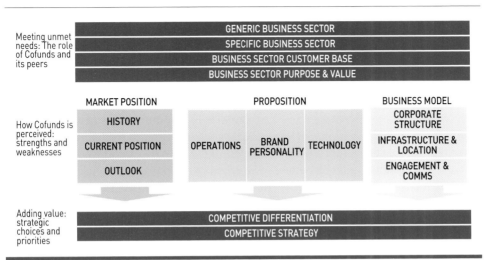

Meeting unmet needs: The role of Cofunds and its peers	GENERIC BUSINESS SECTOR	
	SPECIFIC BUSINESS SECTOR	
	BUSINESS SECTOR CUSTOMER BASE	
	BUSINESS SECTOR PURPOSE & VALUE	

How Cofunds is perceived: strengths and weaknesses

MARKET POSITION — HISTORY, CURRENT POSITION, OUTLOOK

PROPOSITION — OPERATIONS, BRAND PERSONALITY, TECHNOLOGY

BUSINESS MODEL — CORPORATE STRUCTURE, INFRASTRUCTURE & LOCATION, ENGAGEMENT & COMMS

Adding value: strategic choices and priorities — COMPETITIVE DIFFERENTIATION, COMPETITIVE STRATEGY

Source: Merlin Communications, Chase Noble

The research confirmed that the market's perception of the entire platform sector (not just Cofunds) had been undergoing a profound shift. Platforms were increasingly regarded as products rather than a service. When advisers described their relationship with their platform supplier, transactional terms ("useful", "cost-efficient", "reliable") were markedly more frequent than emotional terms ("delight", "surprise", "wonderful").

Cofunds was still respected, but its essence was rooted in the specifics of its operational solution, and its prominent market position, rather than its temperament. Operationally, advisers valued its pragmatic answers to real-life problems: back office integration, asset allocation tools, unbundled pricing and e-data feeds all scored highly. "They steer clear of esoteric niches, and might be a bit clunky in marginal areas," said one respondent. "That's a good thing. It means they're focussing all their firepower on making the basics work flawlessly." Similarly, Cofunds' market position was a positive attribute. They were seen as big and British, possessing a deeply ingrained understanding of the UK market and its players, history, regulation, stakeholders and idiosyncrasies. "They have weight in this market. When they scream, we listen," said one fund house.

Wynne-Jones knew that Cofunds needed to jealously guard these brand values. Operational reliance and market strength are both compelling advantages to stress when encouraging potential customers to make a favourable choice. Nevertheless, he was concerned about what was absent. Advisers no longer seemed to relate to Cofunds' culture. Its personality, once so striking, had faded into the background. Where, he wondered, was the intense empathy and fervour that advisers had expressed when it was the new kid on the block. Could the type of loyalty seen on premier league terraces, or in the moshpit at Glastonbury, or at Glorious Goodwood, be rekindled? "We needed to turn respect into deeply-felt loyalty," says Wynne-Jones. "To recreate a sense of magic."

In an electrifying series of melodramatic announcements, Cofunds seized the initiative. They rebuilt their pricing structure to link fees, costs and value in a more transparent manner. They became more outspoken in the trade media. And they eradicated the final vestiges of an archaic age from their platform processes. One respondent said "they really wanted to understand the processes between different fund managers, and between fund managers and advisers. They deconstructed them, chucked out anything that was superfluous, and only retained the essentials. It's like airline ticketing, where the old ten step process was cut down to about two. That takes a certain obstinate and determined mindset."

Symbolism was conspicuous in Wynne-Jones drive to return the "magic", as seen in Cofunds' revolutionary 'Budget Webinars'. "I remember 15 years ago, before I was at Cofunds, how pleased we were to mail out a Budget digest to clients within a week," he says. "Today we can be so much more ambitious. Within a few hours of the Chancellor's announcements, we host an online Budget webinar discussion." The format reinforces Cofunds' thought leadership, and its positive support for the adviser community. "It doesn't simply regurgitate the raw facts. Those are all over the internet anyway. Instead, we get a panel of experts to extract the key issues, especially where they entail opportunities for advisers and their clients. And it's fully interactive - last time, our audience numbered in the thousands, questions were flying around every few seconds." This simple but high-profile initiative encapsulated many of the facets Wynne-Jones sought to ingrain into the brand: listening, helpful, expert, fast.

When Cofunds repeated the research exercise in 2013, the strides made were evident. Advisers now strongly associated with Cofunds the value of *aspiration* - both for itself, for its immediate customers, and for the wider public. They glimpsed a restlessness, a willingness to reinvent and re-engineer, and an impulse to look forward over the immediate horizon, that is rare in market leaders. "Every year they strive to provide something new, that's more practical and valuable. It's what makes them tick," said a Chartered practitioner in a Hampshire firm. "Great technology and support and expertise are satisfiers," says Wynne-Jones. "Without those, you may as well leave the pitch. But that's not how you win. Our instinct is forever to look to the future, so we can reinvent and re-engineer." For firms with this type of edgy attitude and stubborn psyche, past achievements are of scant value. The Grand Prix driver about to turbocharge his way around Silverstone may fondly remember his childhood scooter, but needs an entirely different toy for the task ahead.

During the research, it emerged that many advisers anticipated an imminent shakeout in the platform sector. Strategically, this would not be unusual. Markets entering their maturity phase often see players depart the field who failed to break through from also-ran status. Respondents predicted rationalisation; some felt a handful of market leaders would pull away from the rest, leaving a squeezed middle, and perhaps a half dozen niche firms. Yet all expected Cofunds would be one of the winners during any such upheaval and consolidation. It had the gusto, loyalty and credibility to see it through stormy times.

As time moved forward, it emerged that advisers were not alone in appreciating the Cofunds story. Shortly after the research concluded, the firm was acquired by insurance giant *Legal & General*, who had been a minority investor since 2005. In announcing the deal, the new parent promised to use their financial muscle, as a top 100 UK public company, to support the continuing journey of this once and future upstart.

WALMART FOUNDER SAM WALTON once said that, "The customer is the ultimate boss ... (the one who) can fire everybody in the company from the chairman on down, simply by spending money somewhere else." Enduring businesses are likely to be preoccupied with delivering compelling value, even (or especially) when it means reforming the Value Chain or restructuring the legacy workings of an entire sector. And, like planets orbiting a star, these strategies will be centred on a brand personality that engages both rationally and emotionally with customers. Value felt in the heart as well as the wallet.

STRATEGY AND THE G-FORCE
Turning teams into champions

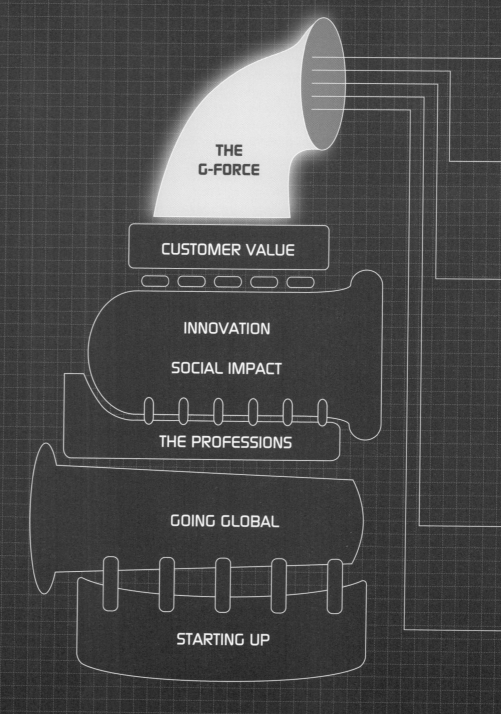

THE
G-FORCE

CUSTOMER VALUE

INNOVATION

SOCIAL IMPACT

THE PROFESSIONS

GOING GLOBAL

STARTING UP

NOT FOR THE FAINT-HEARTED

- Many teams struggle to function
- Dangerous attitudes can lurk unspoken
- The perfect leader has yet to be forged.

AN AMBITION SHARED

- Four types: Year Zero, Ruthless Priorities, New Bets, Continuing Journey
- Input materials – blue sky or grounded?
- Output sought – thematic or SMART?

THE G-FORCE

- Galvanise your skills: Anchorage, preparation, mobilisation, skills audit, roles, working practices
- Generate ideas: Brainstorming, benchmarking, divergence, opening gates, no constraints, possibilities
- Grab the headlines: Decisions, big themes, convergence, captivating, inspiring, discarding the trash
- Get detailed: Market analysis, business model, proposition, benefits, financial plans, operational plans
- Give it wings: Red Bull, flash of genius, innovation, pushing boundaries, being distinctive, excitement
- Go for it: Plan of attack, the team primed, resources marshalled, leadership, measuring delivery, accomplishments.

THE G-FORCE IN ACTION

- Taking ownership
- Sorting out the basics
- Mentoring.

END WORD: FROM TEAMS TO CHAMPIONS

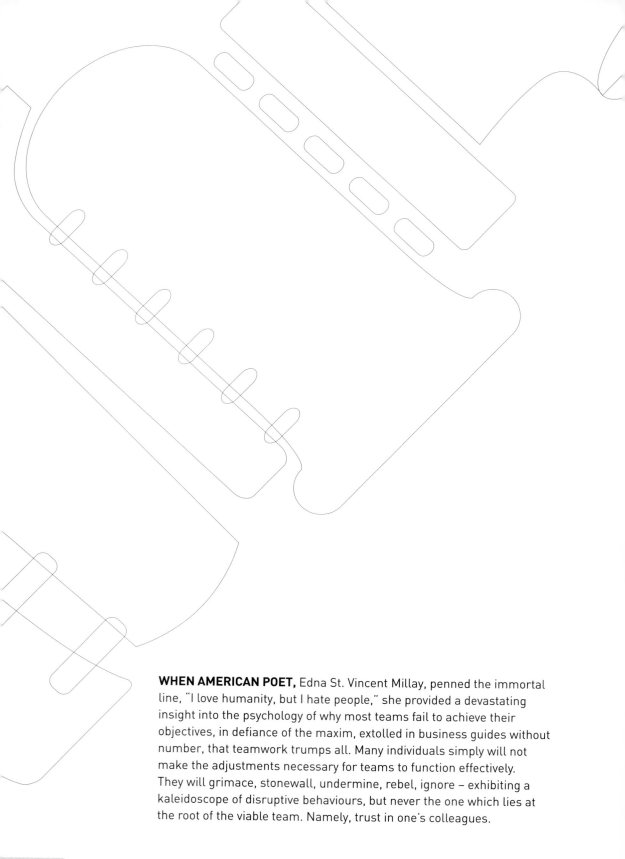

WHEN AMERICAN POET, Edna St. Vincent Millay, penned the immortal line, "I love humanity, but I hate people," she provided a devastating insight into the psychology of why most teams fail to achieve their objectives, in defiance of the maxim, extolled in business guides without number, that teamwork trumps all. Many individuals simply will not make the adjustments necessary for teams to function effectively. They will grimace, stonewall, undermine, rebel, ignore – exhibiting a kaleidoscope of disruptive behaviours, but never the one which lies at the root of the viable team. Namely, trust in one's colleagues.

NOT FOR THE FAINT-HEARTED

Some evolutionary biologists argue that trust runs counter to human nature. It's suggested that any Neanderthal whose instinct was to trust the unfamiliar tribe approaching from the western plains would have met a grisly and blood-soaked end. By contrast, those with a wary and cautious disposition were rewarded with a more bountiful life expectancy. Throughout the ages, Machiavellian plotters have often prospered at the expense of the upright and fastidious. Whether it has been opening trading routes through Persia and onwards to the east, or colonising the newly-discovered Americas in pursuit of territory, minerals, wealth and glory, history has often been written by the most duplicitous and devious leaders whose scruples, if any, were kept firmly under control.

Alan Sugar's series, *The Apprentice*, is Exhibit One for those who believe such traits persevere in business (although perhaps without such graphic butchery of mutineers). The competition commences with fourteen contestants separated into two teams, each tasked to outperform the other in a sales, design, procurement or operations assignment. Within moments, the teams degenerate into an inchoate mass of egos, until the most belligerent character emerges as leader-in-name-only, and strains to exercise a modicum of order upon a half dozen hostile and obstreperous peers, each calculating short-term tactics on the basis of unadulterated, mutually destructive self-interest. Exaggerated slightly under the unforgiving glare of the television camera, the programme speaks to the difficulty of melding individualism with group dynamics to create a positive outcome.

The extravert personalities in *The Apprentice* are vocal in their defiance, but in the workplace often the most dangerous attitudes are unspoken, lurking beneath the surface. Hence they fester unaddressed. Individuals may approach their tasks with trepidation ("I flunked something similar last time"), or self-pity ("I'm always given the thankless stuff"), or paranoia ("they'll fire me if I mess up"), or resentment ("my revenge will be glorious"). All the while, the hapless team leader bumbles along, ignorant of these sentiments, saying the wrong things at the wrong time until the edifice collapses amidst jealousy and recrimination.

In his brilliant treatise *In the Company of Leaders*, Campbell Macpherson deconstructs the leadership styles of the gamut of chief executives under whom he has served, from Mr Excitable to Mr Velcro Hands to Ms Wonder Woman, concluding that the perfect leader has not yet been forged. And, even if such a collage could be assembled, combining the vision of Martin Luther King with the passion of Winston Churchill, the financial acumen of George Soros with the communication skills of Steven Spielberg, a leader is limited to shrill exhortations if the team entire is inadequately bonded.

The bulk of this chapter explores the role that one such bonding agent can perform. The G-Force is a tool that has been developed to galvanise the individual capabilities of team members around a common purpose. Like an adhesive dripping into every pore, it encourages team members to share and collude rather than strain with frustration in incompatible directions. Structured around a sequence of six focused topics, each designed to bring out different skills within the team, it leads remorselessly to a grand crescendo – one to which all team members can make a unique and valued contribution.

AN AMBITION SHARED

Firstly, however, the team's mission must be clear. So let us take a brief detour into the world of the notorious corporate offsite (alternatively known as the awayday, the jamboree, or the jolly). These are occasions, clouded in secrecy to the rest of the organisation, when groups of executives will sequester themselves away in (depending on the budget) a country house hotel, a ship in the Solent, a Regus office, or a basement boxroom. Like cardinals considering the election of the next pope, they will ruminate and cogitate, barter and banter, until they emerge back into the sunlight with missions and messages to extol.

When great matters are at stake, those charged with preparing the Agenda and Format (A&F) of an awayday face rabbit holes aplenty along the pathway. Wine selections, breakout rooms, projectors than won't lose focus, screens that won't collapse, the meaning of 'casual smart' in the dress code instructions – all can be troublesome issues, prone to destabilise the unwary, but they fade into nothingness compared with getting the A&F spot-on. Indeed, a common failing is to assume there is one irrevocable and immutable A&F, suitable for all occasions.

On the contrary, the A&F can take a number of shapes. Since it's enshrined in gold lettering on the front cover of the consultant's Code of Practice that every scenario must be reducible to a 2x2 matrix, these options are depicted using precisely that device in *Figure 7.1*.

This schematic posits that four models exist – plus a bonus fifth – for running a corporate offsite. It defines the models in terms of the nature of the input materials (grounded vs. blue sky), and the output sought (SMART* vs. thematic). Clarification around these issues will determine whether the tone of the offsite is to focus on Year Zero, Ruthless Priorities, New Bets, or the Continuing Journey. Once the organiser is clear about these essentials, the details of the A&F can take a coherent, relevant shape.

* SMART: Specific, Measurable, Achievable, Realistic, Time-bound

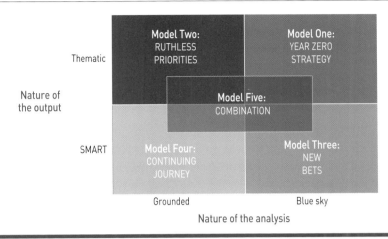

Source: Chase Noble

Model One: Year Zero Strategy
Input materials: Blue sky. Output sought: Thematic.
Under the Year Zero model, the offsite might begin with a wide-ranging and no-holds-barred appraisal of the opportunities and threats presented to the organisation by the external environment, including the health of the market, the expectations and behaviours of customers, the relative power of the Tower of Babel of organisations within the supply chain, the number and strategies of direct and indirect competitors, and the evolving shape of regulation and legislation. Consciously disregarding practical constraints, the meeting might then consider a range of options – some seemingly outlandish, others more restrained – for how the firm might adjust its footprint in this and adjacent markets.

Challenging, testing and scrutinising these options should lead to a coalescing of opinion around strategic choices that may bear little relationship to the inherited direction of travel. New commercial and financial objectives, perhaps even a new vision, could drift like an ascending scuba diver to the surface. For this reason, the Year Zero model is most likely to be adopted by organisations facing a moment of crisis, when doing nothing carries the single, terrifying consequence of guaranteeing corporate demise.

Model Two: Ruthless Priorities
Input materials: Grounded. Output sought: Thematic.
Under the Priority Setting model, the participants may be invited to attend the offsite armed with a sheaf of possible projects and activities in need of resources. The event will then focus remorselessly, and to the exclusion of new thinking, on screening and selecting between these proposals. Effectively, the strategy of the organisation

is disassembled into a series of opportunities, each of which is evaluated on merit, before being approved or discarded, with the survivors reassembled to form the new plan. During this type of awayday, the over-riding concern of the strategist is to return to the rank and file with clear, decisive and focused choices about matters which may perchance have been smoldering, unresolved and unanswered, since times forgotten.

Typically, at the outset, the delegates may agree the assessment criteria they will employ, so that a standard frame of reference exists – for example, the degree to which each project aligns with the vision, the known expectations of key stakeholders, the profile of the anticipated cashflows, the potential downside and so forth. After an initial screening to eliminate outliers, the meeting may embark upon a more thorough dissection of the quarter- and semi-finalists during a second screening round. Once the strategic choices are made, the plan is reformed as the sum total of the projects which warrant the go-ahead, with a final check that the reconstituted plan is balanced and coherent in its entirety.

Model Three: New Bets
Input materials: Blue sky. Output sought: SMART.
Under the New Bets model, the offsite has one over-riding goal. The participants need to emerge ready to place their chips as the wheel starts to spin. This tends to materialise when, collectively, the group feels it has a decent grasp of the unfurling narrative taking place around it. The event may invite an economist, demographer or futurologist to shed light on the years ahead: what will be the state of the global or national economy, where will new demand segments emerge, how will technology revolutionise people's lives, what lifestyles and outlooks will young people bring as they enter the workplace, how will the continuing shift eastwards in the globe's economic centre of gravity affect businesses in different niches?

As they consider such matters, the team will be seeking to create clarity from the morass of often-contradictory indicators. It will lock down what it knows, agree where it's confident in specific beliefs or assumptions, filter what others are telling it, and car park items it could subsequently find out. All these discussions take place in pursuit of a single outcome: where does the team foresee opportunities arising during the planning period? Depending on its degree of risk appetite, and its level of confidence in its predictive prowess, by the conclusion of the offsite the team will feel equipped either to place all its chips on number 25, or spread them more cautiously between reds and blacks and highs and lows.

Model Four: Continuing Journey
Input materials: Grounded. Output sought: SMART.
Under the Continuing Journey model, the team will essentially be engaged in an update to the previous year's plan. This type of event will generally be appropriate when the ship of state is sailing serenely across the waters, and – while modest tacking may be necessary to circumvent a school of playful dolphins – the vessel will remain

firmly on course towards its destination. Perhaps an extensive review has occurred in the recent past, and the task of the strategist is to understand how previous recommendations are taking effect. While the Continuing Journey approach may lack the panache and swagger of the other options, in practice it's the most widespread philosophy. Few management teams, and none that aspire to longevity, will wish to impose a radical upheaval and dramatic about-turn on an annual basis. Like the yo-yo dieter, this would cause lasting damage to its anatomy.

A typical Continuing Journey offsite would begin with a "12 months on" examination of what was previously documented. Part post-mortem, part-celebration, the review would distil which elements of the strategy are soaring, which are working, which are lagging and which are fundamentally off-course. It would re-evaluate the environmental pressures, deducing what has changed, what is new, and where next. And it would use these diagnostic tools to answer, layer by layer, project by project, and workstream by workstream, the fate of each component within the strategy. At the denouement of the event, certain activities may be retained without so much as a spring clean. Some may be granted fresh investment to stimulate more oomph, or be otherwise redirected. New ones may be added. Others may be terminated without mercy. As the dust settles, the new plan will bear many similarities to its forebear, but like a re-upholstered sofa exude a fresh and modern air.

With the Agenda finalised, any strategist charged with facilitating a productive offsite should spend due time considering Format. The theatrical elements of the occasion. Hour piled upon dreary hour of identikit PowerPoint presentations are not the formula for a rousing, sprightly and gratifying debate. Had Windows been in existence when the Brothers Grimm were chronicling their tales, the old fairy need not have resorted to spinning wheels and spindles when plotting how best to cause Rosamond to lose consciousness and fall deep into a 100-year sleep.

As in any halfway decent stage show, monotone pace is verboten. Playwrights know that dramatic scenes are made more intense when they act as a spike after a period of contextualising dialogue. For every stand-up presentation, there should be a period of free-ranging brainstorming. When energy levels are subsiding, departures from script should be encouraged to provide inspiration, refresh creative juices, undermine groupthink, and introduce a new perspective. And the exceptionally brave moderator may on occasion find it irresistible to make full use of the element of surprise to shake away the last cobwebs of complacency. In the early 2011 offsite of an engineering supplies firm with a Europe-wide presence, a 90-minute opening session, ladled with smug pomposity, was brought shuddering to a halt when the chief executive of a major customer emerged from behind the metaphorical arras to deliver uncomfortable truths in forthright terms. The remainder of the event proceeded with a markedly different cadence.

THE G-FORCE

Once the team has its mission, it needs to rise to the challenge. The G-Force (so labelled because of its abundant reliance upon the letter 'G') involves a series of six exercises to achieve precisely this end. Each of the steps is an integral part of the whole; teams cannot bypass or circumvent earlier stages in their rush to the finishing line. Part of the power of the G-Force is that it forces teams to lay solid foundations. Foundations are never the most glamorous part of a prestigious building project. Accolades may fall upon the architects, lighting engineers, sculptors, fit-out gurus, and workplace consultants; the poor souls who diligently laid the foundations rarely benefit from public applause. However, as every novice engineer knows, without foundations the construction will crumble. With this metaphor in mind, let us turn to the six stages of the G-Force, whose six stages – from foundations through to fulfilment – are depicted in *Figure 7.2*.

FIGURE 7.2: Overview of the G-Force

1 Galvanise your skills	2 Generate ideas	3 Grab the headlines	4 Get detailed	5 Give it wings	6 Go for it
Anchorage	Brainstorming	Decisions	Market analysis	Red Bull	Plan of attack
Preparation	Benchmarking	Big themes	Business model	Flash of genius	The team primed
Mobilisation	Divergence	Convergence	Proposition	Innovation	Resources marshalled
Skills audit	Opening gates	Captivating	Benefits	Pushing boundaries	Leadership
Roles	No constraints	Inspiring	Financial plans	Being distinctive	Measuring delivery
Working practices	Possibilities	Discarding the trash	Operational plans	Excitement	Accomplishments

Source: Chase Noble

Step One: Galvanise your skills

The first task is about preparation – anchoring the team and mobilising its members. Without anchorage, the crew will dive for safety at the early signs of an approaching storm. Without anchorage, their vessel will be buffeted about by ever-changing eddies and flows, like a galleon adrift. Teams that race directly into the fray without taking care to prepare will be susceptible to panic and vulnerable to assault. Hurtling ahead can be superficially tempting – it maintains momentum when individuals are pumped up. But progress can be a mirage. Anchorage, on the other hand, creates a secure connection to the ocean floor.

The team debates its objectives until the core purpose is clearly assimilated. Roles are assigned so that all individuals, from team leader downwards, understand how their efforts support the wider purpose. The skills and experiences of the team are audited in light of the activities ahead: where is there a close match, where are there potential clashes, and how will any skill gaps be handled? The team agrees its working practices – will it function as a democracy, a collective, or an autocracy? How will it communicate, how will it reach decisions, how will it deal with issues that arise which have the potential to impair or derail? Distractions are set aside; focus on the task ahead becomes as unbending as the iron flukes of a Herreshoff anchor dug deep into the seabed. With mobilisation complete, the team takes on a hive mindset, congealing, fermenting and finally coalescing around a determined will to succeed. So, anchors aweigh, it can now proceed towards open waters.

Step Two: Generate ideas

Step two is about brainstorming – opening up the range of options that could be harnessed in pursuit of the task. The full spectrum of possibilities can be entertained, from the obvious, safe course, to routes holding out the prospect of a prouder prize albeit at greater risk? The team may game plan a scenario where they are blessed with near limitless resources, and compare it with another in which they are forced to operate under the tightest financial constraints. Should tasks be tackled sequentially, or in parallel? Should the team progress with all-guns-blazin', or work surreptitiously until a riper time? As they gush ideas, they can take inspiration from multiple sources – recent precedents, competitor activities, benchmarks from other sectors, executive statements, shareholder pressure?

The brainstorming stage is not, and should never be, about resolving any of these dilemmas, or closing down discussion. It's about throwing wide open the gates of the Dr Seuss zoo so that everything, from the most docile specimen to the Tizzle-Topped Tufted Mazurka, is available for view. Only later will the team need to arbitrate, select and decide. Where data is weak, it may need to be sourced. Where it's non-existent, it may need to be compiled afresh. But to rush to judgment, bypassing the brainstorming step, could leave many of the best ideas prematurely abandoned before their time. Step two ensures offbeat suggestions with latent potential are not decapitated prior to the exercise of proper scrutiny.

Step Three: Grab the headlines

Step three is the essential complement to the brainstorming exercise. It's about setting out the big themes, to which all else will be subordinate. The 'headline' reference encourages team leaders to think for a moment like a tabloid copywriter who needs to distil a thousand word column into a single bold statement that simultaneously captivates, inspires and intrigues, encouraging the casual reader to delve deeper. With similar brutality, the project team must revisit the hullabaloo of noise and mayhem created during step two, and elicit which few things to elevate above all else.

From *ideas* to *decisions*; from *divergence* to *convergence*; from *everything on the table* to *leftovers discarded with the trash*. In a few succinct and punchy words, perhaps supplemented with a measurable goal ('25 per cent market share', '100,000 customers', 'available from high street retailers by 15 November'), the essence of the mission will be encapsulated. Neither step two, nor step three, is sufficient in isolation, both are essential to enterprise and ambition. Step two alone can leave a team floundering, juggling a myriad of competing priorities, heading in no discernible direction. Step three alone is prone to deliver a middling result, shorn of verve, colour, novelty or innovation. Together, the team can proceed with confidence and tenacity. Confident that it has chosen its strategy for the right, and not the most convenient, reasons. Tenacious because all team members, regardless of role, skills or disposition, are pursuing a clear agenda with a consistent purpose.

Step Four: Get detailed

Up until step three, the team has been operating in the stratosphere, surveying the expanse ahead. It has been fixing the important stuff and painting the broad strokes. Serious business, but perhaps prone to abstraction and remoteness. So, in step four, it's finally time to get personal. The leader forces the team to shift gear, and conceive of the project not as some ethereal grand design, but as it will appear on the ground, when it touches individuals, communities and organisations. The team must now wrestle with its market analysis, its business model, its financial projections, its operating plans.

Some teams may use as their starting point a checklist of all those who will be affected by their work – their shareholders, their customers, their suppliers, their staff, reporters, commentators, regulators, lobbyists. They may itemise all the contact channels that will be created – initial communications, point of sale, service delivery, ongoing support. They may then role play the journey a client will take, dissecting the minutiae of the experience for both the rational and emotional impact. These details will confirm (one hopes) where the team's work plan is delivering a real and appreciable difference to its key stakeholders, those on whose continuing support it relies. Properly executed, this is the stage where the programme starts to matter. It descends from that stratosphere to affect livelihoods. So, for example, if step two gushed the names of a thousand transport contraptions invented throughout history, and step three prioritised the building of a better school bus, now step four must concern itself with the practicalities of ferrying little Penelope and her classmates to arrive at school on time, in comfort and safety.

In step three, detail was an unwanted diversion ("the devil is in the..."). By contrast, in step four, the detail is all that counts ("paying attention to the...").

Step Five: Give it wings

There will come a time when the team needs to lockdown its plans. But before that moment arrives, one final devastating challenge needs to ring out. The team must ask itself whether it has yet sired a Red Bull moment. Is there an element of the work that somehow pushes back the boundaries, stretches the team to go beyond its prior experience, smashes asunder preconceived expectations? Giving it wings could involve an innovative product feature, a distinctive service element, or a memorable catchphrase used in communications. It could simply be delivering results in a way that's faster and more reliable than ever hitherto witnessed in the sector.

Begetting a flash of genius is not always conducive to team harmony and goodwill. For the same reason that the greatest artists and poets are often manic depressives, a team which pushes itself to excel can often experience moods of restlessness, insecurity and frustration. Real progress depends upon eccentrics and brave hearts, not conformists. Teams that find their muse, and conceive a spark of inspiration for their work, are not guaranteed inner fulfilment. Excitement, controversy and the scars of battle are a more likely destiny, and no high performing leader has ever shied away from such a fate.

Step Six: Go for it

By now, the team is mobilised and galvanised. It has explored the universe of options ahead by generating ideas. It has decided the themes that will make it famous through grabbing the headlines. It has ensured its work will positively matter to real individuals by getting detailed and personal. And, by giving wings to its work, it has reached with impatient and lusty ambition for the stars. It's now almost ready to perform. The final task is to gather, organise and then Go For It. The leader entreats the team to assemble all the components from the preceding stages into a single, trenchant plan of attack. A plan in which the tasks have been made crystal clear, individuals primed for their roles, resources marshalled, objectives set and timetables established. Decisive, definitive, delivered.

Like sacred scrolls, the project plan can be a unique point of reference, used to measure, monitor, test and challenge. As this organising exercise nears completion, the leader's mantle of responsibilities takes shape. He or she is the ultimate custodian of the plan. He or she will have signed-off that the mission is worthwhile and the solution is credible. He or she will assign team members to the roles for which they are temperamentally and technically best suited. He or she will agree channels and tools for ongoing dialogue – regular reporting, or 'by exception' reporting, or dashboard reporting. And he or she will ensure that, like a spider balancing at the centre of a vast spiral orb of webbing, they are attuned to any vibrations in the spinnerets that call for immediate response.

In the echoing words of film producers throughout the ages, from Orson Welles to Joss Whedon, it's time for: "Lights, camera, action."

THE G-FORCE IN ACTION

"The purpose of the programme is to help a number of our high-flyers make the step up to the next level," explains Tali Shlomo, the energetic Head of Human Resources at the *Chartered Insurance Institute*. She was the inspiration and driving force behind an initiative that took place in autumn 2013, entitled Enterprise 500. It involved a series of workshops and events over a three-month period, in which participants engaged in a multifaceted series of tasks. "The activities were designed to expose them to many new experiences," says Shlomo. "Team building, commercial thinking, product development, service delivery, presentations, influencing."

At the heart of the exercise was a competition between three teams, each comprising five members of staff, to raise funds for the Prince's Trust – the charity, of which HRH The Prince of Wales is President, that has helped 750,000 young people since 1976 to develop new skills, and gain confidence, so they are better placed to move into work, education or training.

The programme was launched with a full-day workshop during which each team was challenged to create a business idea and plan. Two weeks later, the teams were required to present their plans to senior managers in a *Dragons' Den* environment, where they argued for funding. The programme concluded with a full day event, celebrating the funds raised and reflecting on the lessons learned. Throughout the period, each participant was encouraged to maintain a personal learning log, including short video diary entries, audio reflections and even a blog or Twitter feed.

"The number one principle is about taking ownership," says Shlomo, "both as teams and as individuals. As our rising stars are promoted to positions of greater responsibility, this is one of the main behaviours they must display. They cannot hide behind others when problems need to be tackled. I'm really looking for people to step forward and seize the challenge. Far better to have an idea that doesn't quite work out, than never to try at all."

The kick-off workshop was structured around the six stages of the G-Force methodology. After a brief warm-up exercise in which delegates reviewed examples of entrepreneurship from diverse sectors, they huddled into their teams to Galvanise skills, Generate ideas, Grab the headlines, Get detailed, Give it wings, and Go for it. Throughout, their efforts and energies were geared towards the deliverable of a succinct, targeted, powerful plan to make a reality of their chosen business idea. This was no computer-based simulation or virtual reality exercise; the teams would be bringing a real product to market.

To this end, a planning template was suggested for teams to use as they road-tested the merits of each idea, and to check off the types of actions necessary to bring it to fruition (see *Figure 7.3*). With deference to the pressure of time, and in the interests of laser-like focus, the teams were steered clear of the 500-page business plan genre beloved of corporate Britain. The template consisted of just four sections, with a limit on content of one page per section: the Market Analysis, the Strategic Objectives, the Business Model, and the Action Plans. "By the end of the first day, a few basics had to be sorted," says Shlomo. "Are they clear on their vision and mission? Have they allocated roles and responsibilities? Is there an investment plan? Have they started to work on their Dragons' Den pitch?"

FIGURE 7.3: Business plan template

Market analysis		
	• Market size	• Supply chain
	• Customer segmentation	• Regulation
	• Competitors	• Key opportunity
Strategic objectives		
	• Vision	• Objectives (financial)
	• Core proposition	• Objectives (operational)
	• Positioning	
Business model		
	• Product	• Policies
	• Benefits	• Distribution
	• Added value	
Action plans		
	• Responsibilities	• Website
	• Timelines	• Production
	• Milestones	• Sourcing
	• Resources	• Pricing
	• Measures	• People

Before unleashing such an ambitious programme of personal development, Shlomo added a final element which, she knew, would make sparks fly – like a high school chemistry teacher encouraging the class to throw a smidgeon of dish soap into a beaker containing hydrogen peroxide and potassium iodide (for those whose secondary education is a distant memory, the reaction entails rapid decomposition leading to an eruption of steaming foam and a fair amount of heat).

But instead of introducing a Bunsen burner and periodical table, Shlomo selected a senior executive within the organisation to act as personal mentor to each team, in the full knowledge the individuals could (when provoked) be acerbic and irascible. "I briefed the mentors that, under no circumstance, should they become the surrogate project leader," she insists. "They could provide advice and counsel at the request of the teams, but never assume control." An important challenge for the mentors was to catalyse the teams to think outside familiar organisational silos. "As people advance in their careers, they need to have the skills to access and use resources from elsewhere," says Shlomo. Throughout the programme, mentors were primed to lob hints and reflections that would stimulate team members to reach beyond their local ambit, and cross-fertilise their ideas with support from new, unexpected quarters.

Galvanise your skills – in action. Suzanne Townsend, an experienced marketing operations executive, took charge of team one. "The first task was to create an inventory of the skills around the table," she relates. "And we didn't just limit it to people's job roles. We wanted to know what positions they'd held earlier in their careers. What are their outside interests? Do they have any qualifications from night school that might be relevant?" With the cataloguing complete, Townsend realised the unexpected depth and breadth of talent at her disposal. "We had certain people who were very tech-savvy. And some who understood cashflow and margin analysis. Where we didn't have specific skills in the team, it wasn't difficult to figure out where we could beg or borrow, or call in favours to plug the gap." At that point, the team made a conscious, and bold, decision to avoid the default option of giving specialist tasks to the best-qualified specialist. "We saw this is a fertile opportunity to learn new skills," says Townsend. "So we divided up the responsibilities to take people outside their comfort zones."

Generate ideas – in action. Nicola Pope, a human resources professional with an infectious creative streak, took the reins as team two embarked upon its brainstorm, standing at the flip chart with a marker pen in each hand. "My first words were that no-one should be restrained by practicalities, or nervous to speak in case they were contradicted. That was the basis of gushing as many possible schemes as the page would allow." As the suggestions flooded forth, she divided the sheet into two sections: events, and products and services, and used a mind-map to build successive layers upon the first mentioned ideas. "However outlandish, I'd include them in the mind-map," she explains, "because you never know which ones might lead towards a great insight or conclusion." Aware of the dynamics within the group, she was particularly keen to encourage the less outspoken team members to volunteer their proposals. "There were no right or wrong answers. There was no reason to hold back or allow the extrovert characters to dominate. In the end, I can genuinely say the mind-map was a team effort." *Figure 7.4* reproduces verbatim the content of the flip chart.

Source: Enterprise 500 workshop

Grab the headlines – in action. Joanna Shortt, a determined Project Executive specialising in awarding body development, was instrumental in helping team three whittle down the ragbag of ideas into a single, simple and executable strategy. "Firstly we undertook a pre-screening, knocking out the suggestions that, however worthy, exceeded the parameters of time and funding we'd been set. Next, the ideas which left us feeling apathetic or unexcited were rejected." For Shortt, it was important not simply to respond to the loudest voice. "The selection process was based on criteria and fact; I wanted everyone to feel ownership of the outcome, and that wouldn't happen if people were sidelined during the discussion." In the end, the team's decision was fused together from a number of strands. During step two, ideas had included a book, a cookery class, and celebrity endorsements. Now, each of these semi-formed concepts came together in the shape of a Cook Book. After a whirlwind weekend tracking down celebrity chefs for contributions, recipes were submitted from a veritable A to W (Rachel Allen to Lesley Walters) of household names.

Get detailed – in action. Back in team two, David da Costa, an indefatigable Corporate Development Analyst, was working on the sections of the business plan relating to finances, regulation and sourcing. In this team, the central idea was to produce packs of charity Christmas cards, designed by volunteer artists, for sale through many complementary distribution channels. "When we investigated the sector, the numbers were staggering. 952 million greeting cards are sent each year, with over £1 billion spent on Christmas cards. Where they have a choice, one fifth of consumers prefer charity cards, and while e-cards pose a long-term threat, today they cater for different segments of the marketplace." Many elements of the business model and strategy were driven by insights from this research stage. "From the Greeting Card Association, we learned that 85 per cent of purchasers are female," says da Costa. "This informed a number of our design choices." The plan included monthly cash flows, minimising the need for seed capital in favour of recycling funds as they are generated from sales. "The spreadsheet was more sophisticated than we envisaged at outset. It was filled with assumptions about pricing, manufacturing and volume. And even the £15 it cost us to hire a stall for a few hours at Spitalfields market." When operating within tight margins, nothing could be overlooked.

Give it wings – in action. And back once more to team three. Katie Bowers, a feisty Personal Assistant to one of the organisation's directors, realised more could yet be done to distinguish the Cook Book from the legions of identikit alternatives. "It needed to be interactive," she says. "There may be dozens of cook books on the shelves, but none where purchasers personally know the contributors. It needed to be *by* members of staff (and others known to us), *for* members of staff (and others known to us)." After a blisteringly fast survey to confirm interest (85 per cent positive), the team solicited recipes from almost every member of staff on the payroll. "We didn't care whether or not they were seasonal, or comfort food, or the cuisine of a particular country," says Bowers. "Later editions may carry a theme. For the first volume, we just want them to be good. Beyond that, it's a free-for-all." There are some obvious complexities in soliciting amateur content, for example the team has identified a chef and a food technician to review and quality assure the recipes. But Bowers remains convinced that interactivity will massively broaden the Cook Book's appeal. "How often do you get the chance to see the name and photo and writings of friends and colleagues in print?" she says, "I think that will really catch people's imagination."

Go for it – in action. Jacob Quagliozzi, advertising sales executive extraordinaire, worked within the same team to take the grandiose vision and ensure the plan was delivered on time and to budget. "The timescale was aggressive. Within a couple of months, we had to compile a 32-page book, arrange for 200 to be printed, and raise over £1000 for the Prince's Trust. The action list ran to many pages; there wasn't a hope of success unless we were very focused on getting stuff done." Lines of communication were vital. The team decided to meet formally once or twice each week, and to exchange emails whenever significant developments occurred between meetings. "We rotated the chairing of our get-togethers," says Quagliozzi, "and the chairperson's number one duty was to circulate the agreed actions within an hour or so of its conclusion." Momentum was self-sustaining; Quagliozzi knew that if any one individual grew disenchanted or unreliable, the repercussions would disrupt every other workstream. "That's where our mentor, Kim Glenister (Customer Services Director) was such a blessing. Whenever there was a hint of dawdling or filibustering, she'd offload her blunt observations and get us back on track."

At the time of writing, the Enterprise 500 programme is rapidly approaching the sprint finish and the final audience of the teams with the Dragons. The team leaders are now anticipating that Shlomo's fund-raising targets, which at first seemed light-years beyond reach, will not merely be achieved. By a comfortable margin, they will be transcended.

END WORD: FROM TEAMS TO CHAMPIONS

THE ANCIENT FRATERNITY OF CYNICS has appeared with alarming regularity throughout this narrative, like tenacious badgers poking their heads out through the newly-laid turf that, after the colony's overnight endeavours, resembles an Emmenthal Swiss cheese. Through four series of *Prison Break*, malevolent authority figures sought to deter Michael Schofield (Chapter one). The African Cro-Magnons would never have instigated the Great Leap Forward if they had paid heed to their more risk-averse, lackadaisical brethren (Chapter two). Those instigating a resurgence in professionalism, redefined for a new age, must overcome naysayers and defeatists at every turn (Chapter three). Carping voices hint that new models of social intervention will collapse as readily as the St Paul's Occupy camps (Chapter four). Innovators must close their ears to pessimists who see the next Apollo 1 launch pad fire in every suggestion to experiment and improvise (Chapter five). And, I fear, the spirit of the deputy ambassador still flaunts its callous insouciance through the attitudes and behaviours of many who are meant to provide a customer service (Chapter six).

And cynics also parade their doubts about the effective workings of teams. Harvey Robbins was voicing a widely-held prejudice when he wrote that, "Teams are trouble, because they're made of people, and people are trouble," in his polemic treatise *Why Teams Don't Work*.

The cynics may bewail and lament and deplore. But they will not triumph. Not if teams – working perchance in start-ups, in global enterprises, or in the professions, and delivering perchance a social impact, or innovation, or customer value – are prepared to take the initiative. In these seven chapters, I have drawn on personal observations over three decades, on the experiences of leading practitioners from a multitude of organisations and sectors, and on the writings of esteemed business academics who make a living from extracting trends and themes. As I have delved into each topic, I have sought to identify some essential Pivot Points which, I trust, will assist every budding strategist tasked to navigate a distinctive path through the thickets ahead.

But none of these Pivot Points will matter if teams are characterised by suspicion, recrimination and conflict. That's why the conclusions of this final chapter are the most far-reaching of all. Only when a team is able to Galvanise its skills, Generate ideas, Grab the headlines, Get detailed, Give it wings and Go for it, can it move from lethargic to legendary performance. So let's reveal the cynics as false prophets. Switch on the turbocharged engine. Allow the compressor to draw in the ambient air and pump it vigorously into the combustion chamber, increasing the power potential in the way the G-Force (coupled with a mid-morning espresso) unleashes a project team.

TurboCharged, our teams will be more than assemblies of random individuals investing the minimum effort to avoid summary dismissal. They will be transformed into something altogether more mighty and marvellous. From teams to winners. To world-beaters. To champions.

BIBLIOGRAPHY

Chapter 1: Strategy and starting up

- Ghosh, Shikhar, *Why Companies Fail – and How Their Founders Can Bounce Back*, Harvard Business School Working Knowledge, 2011
- Hill, Terry, *Small Business*, Macmillan Small Business Series, 1987
- Robinson, Jeffrey, *The Risk Takers: Portraits of Money, Ego and Power*, Unwin, 1985
- Wicks, Simon, *Quarterly Survey: Where do Start-Ups and Growing Businesses Find Support?*, Enterprise Nation, May 2013

Chapter 2: Strategy and going global

- Bryan, Lowell and Diana Farrell, *Market Unbound: Unleashing Global Capitalism*, John Wiley, 1996
- Diamond, Jared, *Guns, Germs and Steel: A Short History of Everybody for the Last 13,000 Years*, Vintage, 1998
- International Monetary Fund, *The Fund's Role Regarding Cross-Border Capital Flows*, approved by Reza Moghadam and Sean Hagan, November 2010
- International Monetary Fund, *Understanding Financial Interconnectedness*, approved by Reza Moghadam and Jose Vinals, October 2010
- Isaacson, Walter, *Steve Jobs: The Exclusive Biography*, Little, Brown, 2011
- Real Capital Analytics, *Global Capital Trends: 2011 Year In Review*, 2012
- Reed, Arthur, *Airline*, BBC Books, 1990
- Roxburg, Charles, Susan Land and John Piotrowski, McKinsey Global Institute, *Mapping Global Capital Markets 2011*
- Smith, Laurence and David Wolfe, *Support Departments as a Source of Corporate Profit Improvement*, Prime Strategy Position Paper, 1992
- Toffler, Alvin, *Future Shock*, Pan Books, 1970

Chapter 3: Strategy and the professions

- ACCA: Association of Chartered Certified Accountants, *The Complete Finance Professional: Why Breadth and Depth of Finance Capability Matter in Today's Finance Function*, 2013
- Chase Noble, *Attitudes to Professionalism*, an unpublished research report based on consumer and SME focus groups, 2013
- Chartered Institute of Purchasing and Supply; *80:20 Vision: What do the Next Two Decades Hold for the Profession?*, 2012
- Chartered Insurance Institute, *The Future of Corporate Chartered Titles: A Consultation*, 2013

Chapter 4: Strategy and social impact

- Brown, Adrian and Will Norman, *Lighting the Touchpaper: Growing the Market for Social Investment in England*, Boston Consulting Group and the Young Foundation, November 2011
- CapGemini and Merrill Lynch, *World Wealth Report*, 2012
- Collins, Jim, and Jerry Porras, *Built To Last: Successful Habits of Visionary Companies*, Random House, 1994
- HM Government, *Growing the Social Investment Market*, July 2012
- Hornsby, Adrian, *The Good Analyst*, Investing For Good, 2012

- Joy, Iona, Lucy de Las Casas, and Benedict Rickley, *Understanding the Demand for and Supply of Social Finance*, The Big Society Finance Fund, April 2011
- Lawson, Dominic, 'Responsible Firms are Really Just Stealing', in *the Sunday Times*, 26 February 2012
- Monitor Institute, *Investing For Social and Environmental Impact*, 2009
- Network Rail, *Sustainable Development Strategy: A Railway Fit For the Future*, 2013
- Shanmugalinga, Cynthia, with Jack Graham, Simon Tucker, Geoff Mulgan, *Growing Social Ventures*, NESTA Policy Paper, February 2011
- Suter, Rhiannon, Susan Scott-Parker and Simon Zadek, *Realising Potential: Disability Confidence Builds Better Business*, Business Disability Forum, undated

Chapter 5: Strategy and innovation

- Brown, Stuart, and Christopher Vaughan, *Play: How It Shapes the Brain, Opens the Imagination, and Invigorates the Soul*, J P Tarcher/Penguin Putnam, 2010
- Chaikin, Andrew, *A Man On The Moon: The Voyages Of The Apollo Astronauts*, Michael Joseph, 1994
- Chan Kim, W and Renee Mauborgne, *Creating New Market Space*, Harvard Business Review On Point, 2004
- Clayton Christenson, *The Innovator's Dilemma: When new Technologies Cause Great Firms to Fail*, Harvard Business School Press, 1997
- Drucker, Peter, *Innovation and Entrepreneurship*, Butterworth-Heinemann, 2007
- Grotzinger, John, 'Field Trip to Mars', in *National Geographic*, July 2013
- Kalish, Ira, *Global Power of the Consumer Products Industry*, Deloitte Touche Tohmatsu Limited, 2013
- Kwoh, Leslie, 'You Call That Innovation?' in *the Wall Street Journal*, 23 May 2012

Chapter 6: Strategy and customer value

- Champy, James and Nitin Nohria, *Fast Forward*, Harvard Business Review Books, 1988
- De Bono, Edward, *I Am Right You Are Wrong*, Viking, 1990
- Doyle, Peter, *Marketing Management and Strategy*, Prentice Hall, 1994
- Kay, John, *Obliquity: Why Our Goals are Best Achieved Indirectly*, Penguin Press, 2010
- Rappaport, Alfred, *Creating Shareholder Value: The New Standard for Business Performance*, The Free Press, 1986

Chapter 7: Strategy and the G-Force

- Macpherson, Campbell, *In The Company Of Leaders*, Campbell Macpherson & Associates
- Robbins, Harvey and Michael Finley, *Why Teams Don't Work*, Texere, 2000
- Smith, Laurence, *Why Strategies Fail*, Chase Noble Management Guides, 2012

chasenoble

Chase Noble helps clients survive and thrive during uncertain times.

Consultancy
Delivering game-changing strategies for market leaders.

Research
Revealing fresh insights into the needs and expectations of stakeholders.

Publishing
Management guides exploring new 21st century challenges.

Mentoring and coaching
Working with high fliers to achieve audacious personal goals.

Training
Practical workshops on the application of strategy principles in the real world.

Facilitation
Interactive strategy sessions with executive teams from the board to the frontline.

Keynote speaking
Exploring themes through a powerful cocktail of insight and entertainment.

Chase Noble Ltd
Audley House
Brimpton Common
Berkshire RG7 4RT
Tel: +44 (0) 119 982 1074
www.chasenoble.com